Philosophy in the Islamic World: A Very Short Introduction

VERY SHORT INTRODUCTIONS are for anyone wanting a stimulating and accessible way into a new subject. They are written by experts, and have been translated into more than 40 different languages.

The series began in 1995, and now covers a wide variety of topics in every discipline. The VSI library now contains over 400 volumes—a Very Short Introduction to everything from Psychology and Philosophy of Science to American History and Relativity—and continues to grow in every subject area.

Very Short Introductions available now:

ACCOUNTING Christopher Nobes
ADVERTISING Winston Fletcher
AFRICAN AMERICAN RELIGION Eddie S. Glaude Jr.
AFRICAN HISTORY John Parker and Richard Rathbone
AFRICAN RELIGIONS Jacob K. Olupona
AGNOSTICISM Robin Le Poidevin
ALEXANDER THE GREAT Hugh Bowden
AMERICAN HISTORY Paul S. Boyer
AMERICAN IMMIGRATION David A. Gerber
AMERICAN LEGAL HISTORY G. Edward White
AMERICAN POLITICAL HISTORY Donald Critchlow
AMERICAN POLITICAL PARTIES AND ELECTIONS L. Sandy Maisel
AMERICAN POLITICS Richard M. Valelly
THE AMERICAN PRESIDENCY Charles O. Jones
THE AMERICAN REVOLUTION Robert J. Allison
AMERICAN SLAVERY Heather Andrea Williams
THE AMERICAN WEST Stephen Aron
AMERICAN WOMEN'S HISTORY Susan Ware
ANAESTHESIA Aidan O'Donnell
ANARCHISM Colin Ward
ANCIENT ASSYRIA Karen Radner
ANCIENT EGYPT Ian Shaw
ANCIENT EGYPTIAN ART AND ARCHITECTURE Christina Riggs
ANCIENT GREECE Paul Cartledge
THE ANCIENT NEAR EAST Amanda H. Podany
ANCIENT PHILOSOPHY Julia Annas
ANCIENT WARFARE Harry Sidebottom
ANGELS David Albert Jones
ANGLICANISM Mark Chapman
THE ANGLO-SAXON AGE John Blair
THE ANIMAL KINGDOM Peter Holland
ANIMAL RIGHTS David DeGrazia
THE ANTARCTIC Klaus Dodds
ANTISEMITISM Steven Beller
ANXIETY Daniel Freeman and Jason Freeman
THE APOCRYPHAL GOSPELS Paul Foster
ARCHAEOLOGY Paul Bahn
ARCHITECTURE Andrew Ballantyne
ARISTOCRACY William Doyle
ARISTOTLE Jonathan Barnes
ART HISTORY Dana Arnold
ART THEORY Cynthia Freeland
ASTROBIOLOGY David C. Catling
ATHEISM Julian Baggini
AUGUSTINE Henry Chadwick
AUSTRALIA Kenneth Morgan
AUTISM Uta Frith
THE AVANT GARDE David Cottington
THE AZTECS Davíd Carrasco
BACTERIA Sebastian G. B. Amyes
BARTHES Jonathan Culler
THE BEATS David Sterritt
BEAUTY Roger Scruton
BESTSELLERS John Sutherland

THE BIBLE John Riches
BIBLICAL ARCHAEOLOGY Eric H. Cline
BIOGRAPHY Hermione Lee
THE BLUES Elijah Wald
THE BOOK OF MORMON Terryl Givens
BORDERS Alexander C. Diener and Joshua Hagen
THE BRAIN Michael O'Shea
THE BRITISH CONSTITUTION Martin Loughlin
THE BRITISH EMPIRE Ashley Jackson
BRITISH POLITICS Anthony Wright
BUDDHA Michael Carrithers
BUDDHISM Damien Keown
BUDDHIST ETHICS Damien Keown
BYZANTIUM Peter Sarris
CANCER Nicholas James
CAPITALISM James Fulcher
CATHOLICISM Gerald O'Collins
CAUSATION Stephen Mumford and Rani Lill Anjum
THE CELL Terence Allen and Graham Cowling
THE CELTS Barry Cunliffe
CHAOS Leonard Smith
CHEMISTRY Peter Atkins
CHILD PSYCHOLOGY Usha Goswami
CHILDREN'S LITERATURE Kimberley Reynolds
CHINESE LITERATURE Sabina Knight
CHOICE THEORY Michael Allingham
CHRISTIAN ART Beth Williamson
CHRISTIAN ETHICS D. Stephen Long
CHRISTIANITY Linda Woodhead
CITIZENSHIP Richard Bellamy
CIVIL ENGINEERING David Muir Wood
CLASSICAL LITERATURE William Allan
CLASSICAL MYTHOLOGY Helen Morales
CLASSICS Mary Beard and John Henderson
CLAUSEWITZ Michael Howard
CLIMATE Mark Maslin
THE COLD WAR Robert McMahon
COLONIAL AMERICA Alan Taylor
COLONIAL LATIN AMERICAN LITERATURE Rolena Adorno
COMEDY Matthew Bevis
COMMUNISM Leslie Holmes
COMPLEXITY John H. Holland
THE COMPUTER Darrel Ince
CONFUCIANISM Daniel K. Gardner
THE CONQUISTADORS Matthew Restall and Felipe Fernández-Armesto
CONSCIENCE Paul Strohm
CONSCIOUSNESS Susan Blackmore
CONTEMPORARY ART Julian Stallabrass
CONTEMPORARY FICTION Robert Eaglestone
CONTINENTAL PHILOSOPHY Simon Critchley
CORAL REEFS Charles Sheppard
CORPORATE SOCIAL RESPONSIBILITY Jeremy Moon
CORRUPTION Leslie Holmes
COSMOLOGY Peter Coles
CRIME FICTION Richard Bradford
CRIMINAL JUSTICE Julian V. Roberts
CRITICAL THEORY Stephen Eric Bronner
THE CRUSADES Christopher Tyerman
CRYPTOGRAPHY Fred Piper and Sean Murphy
THE CULTURAL REVOLUTION Richard Curt Kraus
DADA AND SURREALISM David Hopkins
DANTE Peter Hainsworth and David Robey
DARWIN Jonathan Howard
THE DEAD SEA SCROLLS Timothy Lim
DEMOCRACY Bernard Crick
DERRIDA Simon Glendinning
DESCARTES Tom Sorell
DESERTS Nick Middleton
DESIGN John Heskett
DEVELOPMENTAL BIOLOGY Lewis Wolpert
THE DEVIL Darren Oldridge
DIASPORA Kevin Kenny
DICTIONARIES Lynda Mugglestone
DINOSAURS David Norman
DIPLOMACY Joseph M. Siracusa
DOCUMENTARY FILM Patricia Aufderheide
DREAMING J. Allan Hobson
DRUGS Leslie Iversen
DRUIDS Barry Cunliffe
EARLY MUSIC Thomas Forrest Kelly
THE EARTH Martin Redfern

ECONOMICS Partha Dasgupta
EDUCATION Gary Thomas
EGYPTIAN MYTH Geraldine Pinch
EIGHTEENTH-CENTURY BRITAIN Paul Langford
THE ELEMENTS Philip Ball
EMOTION Dylan Evans
EMPIRE Stephen Howe
ENGELS Terrell Carver
ENGINEERING David Blockley
ENGLISH LITERATURE Jonathan Bate
THE ENLIGHTENMENT John Robertson
ENTREPRENEURSHIP Paul Westhead and Mike Wright
ENVIRONMENTAL ECONOMICS Stephen Smith
EPIDEMIOLOGY Rodolfo Saracci
ETHICS Simon Blackburn
ETHNOMUSICOLOGY Timothy Rice
THE ETRUSCANS Christopher Smith
THE EUROPEAN UNION John Pinder and Simon Usherwood
EVOLUTION Brian and Deborah Charlesworth
EXISTENTIALISM Thomas Flynn
EXPLORATION Stewart A. Weaver
THE EYE Michael Land
FAMILY LAW Jonathan Herring
FASCISM Kevin Passmore
FASHION Rebecca Arnold
FEMINISM Margaret Walters
FILM Michael Wood
FILM MUSIC Kathryn Kalinak
THE FIRST WORLD WAR Michael Howard
FOLK MUSIC Mark Slobin
FOOD John Krebs
FORENSIC PSYCHOLOGY David Canter
FORENSIC SCIENCE Jim Fraser
FORESTS Jaboury Ghazoul
FOSSILS Keith Thomson
FOUCAULT Gary Gutting
FRACTALS Kenneth Falconer
FREE SPEECH Nigel Warburton
FREE WILL Thomas Pink
FRENCH LITERATURE John D. Lyons
THE FRENCH REVOLUTION William Doyle
FREUD Anthony Storr
FUNDAMENTALISM Malise Ruthven
GALAXIES John Gribbin
GALILEO Stillman Drake
GAME THEORY Ken Binmore
GANDHI Bhikhu Parekh
GENES Jonathan Slack
GENIUS Andrew Robinson
GEOGRAPHY John Matthews and David Herbert
GEOPOLITICS Klaus Dodds
GERMAN LITERATURE Nicholas Boyle
GERMAN PHILOSOPHY Andrew Bowie
GLOBAL CATASTROPHES Bill McGuire
GLOBAL ECONOMIC HISTORY Robert C. Allen
GLOBALIZATION Manfred Steger
GOD John Bowker
THE GOTHIC Nick Groom
GOVERNANCE Mark Bevir
THE GREAT DEPRESSION AND THE NEW DEAL Eric Rauchway
HABERMAS James Gordon Finlayson
HAPPINESS Daniel M. Haybron
HEGEL Peter Singer
HEIDEGGER Michael Inwood
HERODOTUS Jennifer T. Roberts
HIEROGLYPHS Penelope Wilson
HINDUISM Kim Knott
HISTORY John H. Arnold
THE HISTORY OF ASTRONOMY Michael Hoskin
THE HISTORY OF LIFE Michael Benton
THE HISTORY OF MATHEMATICS Jacqueline Stedall
THE HISTORY OF MEDICINE William Bynum
THE HISTORY OF TIME Leofranc Holford-Strevens
HIV/AIDS Alan Whiteside
HOBBES Richard Tuck
HORMONES Martin Luck
HUMAN ANATOMY Leslie Klenerman
HUMAN EVOLUTION Bernard Wood
HUMAN RIGHTS Andrew Clapham
HUMANISM Stephen Law
HUME A. J. Ayer
HUMOUR Noël Carroll
THE ICE AGE Jamie Woodward
IDEOLOGY Michael Freeden
INDIAN PHILOSOPHY Sue Hamilton

INFECTIOUS DISEASE Marta L. Wayne and Benjamin M. Bolker
INFORMATION Luciano Floridi
INNOVATION Mark Dodgson and David Gann
INTELLIGENCE Ian J. Deary
INTERNATIONAL MIGRATION Khalid Koser
INTERNATIONAL RELATIONS Paul Wilkinson
INTERNATIONAL SECURITY Christopher S. Browning
IRAN Ali M. Ansari
ISLAM Malise Ruthven
ISLAMIC HISTORY Adam Silverstein
ITALIAN LITERATURE Peter Hainsworth and David Robey
JESUS Richard Bauckham
JOURNALISM Ian Hargreaves
JUDAISM Norman Solomon
JUNG Anthony Stevens
KABBALAH Joseph Dan
KAFKA Ritchie Robertson
KANT Roger Scruton
KEYNES Robert Skidelsky
KIERKEGAARD Patrick Gardiner
KNOWLEDGE Jennifer Nagel
THE KORAN Michael Cook
LANDSCAPE ARCHITECTURE Ian H. Thompson
LANDSCAPES AND GEOMORPHOLOGY Andrew Goudie and Heather Viles
LANGUAGES Stephen R. Anderson
LATE ANTIQUITY Gillian Clark
LAW Raymond Wacks
THE LAWS OF THERMODYNAMICS Peter Atkins
LEADERSHIP Keith Grint
LIBERALISM Michael Freeden
LINCOLN Allen C. Guelzo
LINGUISTICS Peter Matthews
LITERARY THEORY Jonathan Culler
LOCKE John Dunn
LOGIC Graham Priest
LOVE Ronald de Sousa
MACHIAVELLI Quentin Skinner
MADNESS Andrew Scull
MAGIC Owen Davies
MAGNA CARTA Nicholas Vincent
MAGNETISM Stephen Blundell
MALTHUS Donald Winch
MANAGEMENT John Hendry
MAO Delia Davin
MARINE BIOLOGY Philip V. Mladenov
THE MARQUIS DE SADE John Phillips
MARTIN LUTHER Scott H. Hendrix
MARTYRDOM Jolyon Mitchell
MARX Peter Singer
MATERIALS Christopher Hall
MATHEMATICS Timothy Gowers
THE MEANING OF LIFE Terry Eagleton
MEDICAL ETHICS Tony Hope
MEDICAL LAW Charles Foster
MEDIEVAL BRITAIN John Gillingham and Ralph A. Griffiths
MEDIEVAL LITERATURE Elaine Treharne
MEMORY Jonathan K. Foster
METAPHYSICS Stephen Mumford
MICHAEL FARADAY Frank A. J. L. James
MICROBIOLOGY Nicholas P. Money
MICROECONOMICS Avinash Dixit
MICROSCOPY Terence Allen
THE MIDDLE AGES Miri Rubin
MINERALS David Vaughan
MODERN ART David Cottington
MODERN CHINA Rana Mitter
MODERN FRANCE Vanessa R. Schwartz
MODERN IRELAND Senia Pašeta
MODERN JAPAN Christopher Goto-Jones
MODERN LATIN AMERICAN LITERATURE Roberto González Echevarría
MODERN WAR Richard English
MODERNISM Christopher Butler
MOLECULES Philip Ball
THE MONGOLS Morris Rossabi
MORMONISM Richard Lyman Bushman
MOUNTAINS Martin F. Price
MUHAMMAD Jonathan A. C. Brown
MULTICULTURALISM Ali Rattansi
MUSIC Nicholas Cook
MYTH Robert A. Segal
THE NAPOLEONIC WARS Mike Rapport
NATIONALISM Steven Grosby
NELSON MANDELA Elleke Boehmer
NEOLIBERALISM Manfred Steger and Ravi Roy

NETWORKS Guido Caldarelli and Michele Catanzaro
THE NEW TESTAMENT Luke Timothy Johnson
THE NEW TESTAMENT AS LITERATURE Kyle Keefer
NEWTON Robert Iliffe
NIETZSCHE Michael Tanner
NINETEENTH-CENTURY BRITAIN Christopher Harvie and H. C. G. Matthew
THE NORMAN CONQUEST George Garnett
NORTH AMERICAN INDIANS Theda Perdue and Michael D. Green
NORTHERN IRELAND Marc Mulholland
NOTHING Frank Close
NUCLEAR PHYSICS Frank Close
NUCLEAR POWER Maxwell Irvine
NUCLEAR WEAPONS Joseph M. Siracusa
NUMBERS Peter M. Higgins
NUTRITION David A. Bender
OBJECTIVITY Stephen Gaukroger
THE OLD TESTAMENT Michael D. Coogan
THE ORCHESTRA D. Kern Holoman
ORGANIZATIONS Mary Jo Hatch
PAGANISM Owen Davies
THE PALESTINIAN-ISRAELI CONFLICT Martin Bunton
PARTICLE PHYSICS Frank Close
PAUL E. P. Sanders
PEACE Oliver P. Richmond
PENTECOSTALISM William K. Kay
THE PERIODIC TABLE Eric R. Scerri
PHILOSOPHY Edward Craig
PHILOSOPHY IN THE ISLAMIC WORLD Peter Adamson
PHILOSOPHY OF LAW Raymond Wacks
PHILOSOPHY OF SCIENCE Samir Okasha
PHOTOGRAPHY Steve Edwards
PHYSICAL CHEMISTRY Peter Atkins
PILGRIMAGE Ian Reader
PLAGUE Paul Slack
PLANETS David A. Rothery
PLANTS Timothy Walker
PLATE TECTONICS Peter Molnar
PLATO Julia Annas
POLITICAL PHILOSOPHY David Miller
POLITICS Kenneth Minogue
POSTCOLONIALISM Robert Young
POSTMODERNISM Christopher Butler
POSTSTRUCTURALISM Catherine Belsey
PREHISTORY Chris Gosden
PRESOCRATIC PHILOSOPHY Catherine Osborne
PRIVACY Raymond Wacks
PROBABILITY John Haigh
PROGRESSIVISM Walter Nugent
PROTESTANTISM Mark A. Noll
PSYCHIATRY Tom Burns
PSYCHOANALYSIS Daniel Pick
PSYCHOLOGY Gillian Butler and Freda McManus
PSYCHOTHERAPY Tom Burns and Eva Burns-Lundgren
PURITANISM Francis J. Bremer
THE QUAKERS Pink Dandelion
QUANTUM THEORY John Polkinghorne
RACISM Ali Rattansi
RADIOACTIVITY Claudio Tuniz
RASTAFARI Ennis B. Edmonds
THE REAGAN REVOLUTION Gil Troy
REALITY Jan Westerhoff
THE REFORMATION Peter Marshall
RELATIVITY Russell Stannard
RELIGION IN AMERICA Timothy Beal
THE RENAISSANCE Jerry Brotton
RENAISSANCE ART Geraldine A. Johnson
REVOLUTIONS Jack A. Goldstone
RHETORIC Richard Toye
RISK Baruch Fischhoff and John Kadvany
RITUAL Barry Stephenson
RIVERS Nick Middleton
ROBOTICS Alan Winfield
ROMAN BRITAIN Peter Salway
THE ROMAN EMPIRE Christopher Kelly
THE ROMAN REPUBLIC David M. Gwynn
ROMANTICISM Michael Ferber
ROUSSEAU Robert Wokler
RUSSELL A. C. Grayling
RUSSIAN HISTORY Geoffrey Hosking
RUSSIAN LITERATURE Catriona Kelly
THE RUSSIAN REVOLUTION S. A. Smith

SCHIZOPHRENIA Chris Frith and Eve Johnstone
SCHOPENHAUER Christopher Janaway
SCIENCE AND RELIGION Thomas Dixon
SCIENCE FICTION David Seed
THE SCIENTIFIC REVOLUTION Lawrence M. Principe
SCOTLAND Rab Houston
SEXUALITY Véronique Mottier
SIKHISM Eleanor Nesbitt
THE SILK ROAD James A. Millward
SLEEP Steven W. Lockley and Russell G. Foster
SOCIAL AND CULTURAL ANTHROPOLOGY John Monaghan and Peter Just
SOCIAL PSYCHOLOGY Richard J. Crisp
SOCIAL WORK Sally Holland and Jonathan Scourfield
SOCIALISM Michael Newman
SOCIOLINGUISTICS John Edwards
SOCIOLOGY Steve Bruce
SOCRATES C. C. W. Taylor
THE SOVIET UNION Stephen Lovell
THE SPANISH CIVIL WAR Helen Graham
SPANISH LITERATURE Jo Labanyi
SPINOZA Roger Scruton
SPIRITUALITY Philip Sheldrake
SPORT Mike Cronin
STARS Andrew King
STATISTICS David J. Hand
STEM CELLS Jonathan Slack
STRUCTURAL ENGINEERING David Blockley
STUART BRITAIN John Morrill
SUPERCONDUCTIVITY Stephen Blundell
SYMMETRY Ian Stewart
TAXATION Stephen Smith
TEETH Peter S. Ungar
TERRORISM Charles Townshend
THEATRE Marvin Carlson
THEOLOGY David F. Ford
THOMAS AQUINAS Fergus Kerr
THOUGHT Tim Bayne
TIBETAN BUDDHISM Matthew T. Kapstein
TOCQUEVILLE Harvey C. Mansfield
TRAGEDY Adrian Poole
THE TROJAN WAR Eric H. Cline
TRUST Katherine Hawley
THE TUDORS John Guy
TWENTIETH-CENTURY BRITAIN Kenneth O. Morgan
THE UNITED NATIONS Jussi M. Hanhimäki
THE U.S. CONGRESS Donald A. Ritchie
THE U.S. SUPREME COURT Linda Greenhouse
UTOPIANISM Lyman Tower Sargent
THE VIKINGS Julian Richards
VIRUSES Dorothy H. Crawford
WATER John Finney
WILLIAM SHAKESPEARE Stanley Wells
WITCHCRAFT Malcolm Gaskill
WITTGENSTEIN A. C. Grayling
WORK Stephen Fineman
WORLD MUSIC Philip Bohlman
THE WORLD TRADE ORGANIZATION Amrita Narlikar
WORLD WAR II Gerhard L. Weinberg
WRITING AND SCRIPT Andrew Robinson

Available soon:

LIGHT Ian Walmsley
BLACK HOLES Katherine Blundell
HERMENEUTICS Jens Zimmermann
ALGEBRA Peter M. Higgins
INTERNATIONAL LAW Vaughan Lowe

For more information visit our website

www.oup.com/vsi/

Peter Adamson

PHILOSOPHY IN THE ISLAMIC WORLD

A Very Short Introduction

OXFORD
UNIVERSITY PRESS

OXFORD
UNIVERSITY PRESS

Great Clarendon Street, Oxford, OX2 6DP,
United Kingdom

Oxford University Press is a department of the University of Oxford. It furthers the University's objective of excellence in research, scholarship, and education by publishing worldwide. Oxford is a registered trade mark of Oxford University Press in the UK and in certain other countries

First edition published in 2015

Published in the United States of America by Oxford University Press
198 Madison Avenue, New York, NY 10016, United States of America

British Library Cataloguing in Publication Data
Data available

Library of Congress Control Number: 2015937779

ISBN 978–0–19–968367–3

Printed and bound by
CPI Group (UK) Ltd, Croydon, CR0 4YY

Contents

List of illustrations

List of maps

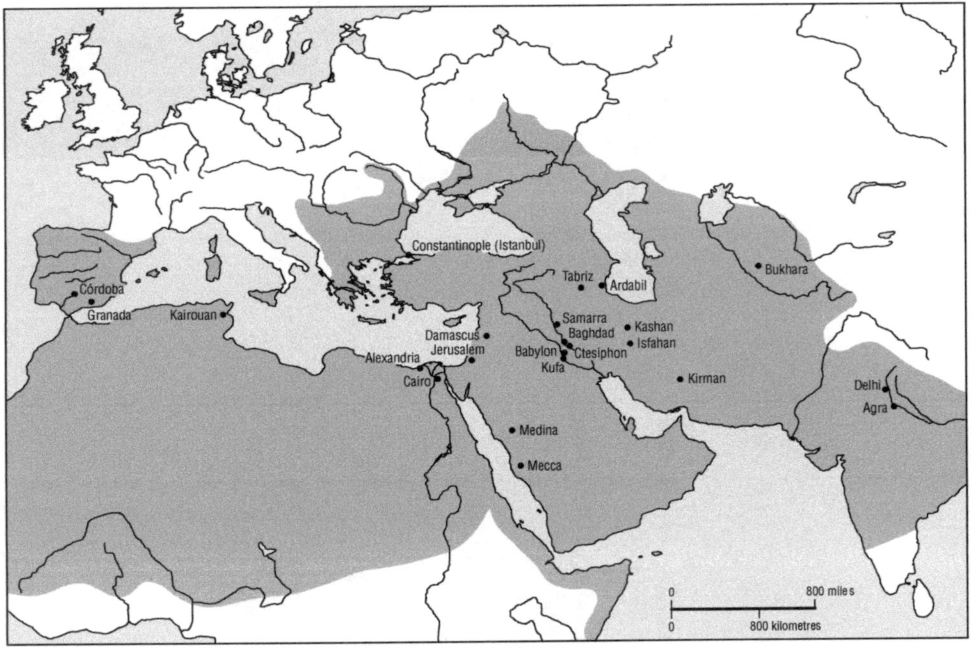

Map 1. Expansion of the Islamic world to 1500.

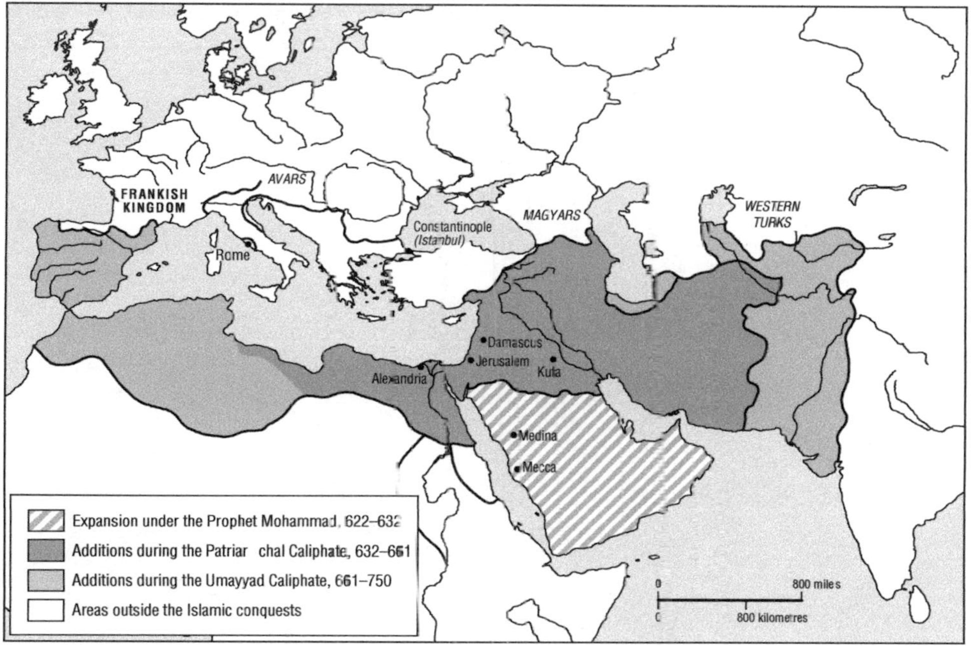

Map 2. Expansion of the Islamic caliphate.

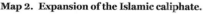

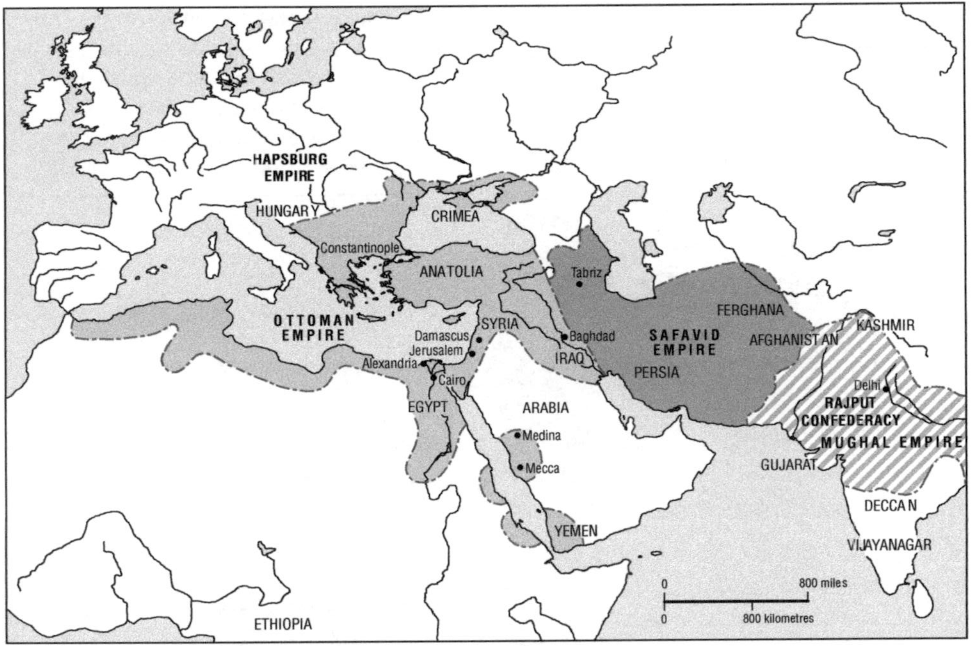

Map 3. The Ottoman, Safavid, and Mughal empires.

Introduction

Why 'philosophy in the Islamic world', and not simply 'Islamic philosophy'? There would have been other options too: 'Arabic philosophy', or even 'Islamicate philosophy'. The last of these would be perfect, if only 'Islamicate' were a real word. It was invented in recent decades to express what I mean by 'the Islamic world', which is to say, the geographical areas that have fallen within Islamic political and cultural control, from the rise of Islam down to the present. But I don't think it has caught on enough to be used in a book title. Neither 'Islamic' nor 'Arabic' philosophy fits the bill either. The trouble with 'Islamic philosophy' is that many important philosophers in the Islamic world were not Muslims. Christian thinkers played a major role in the initial reception and interpretation of Hellenic philosophy, and some of the greatest Jewish philosophers of all time—above all Maimonides—lived and worked in the Islamic world, especially in Muslim Spain. 'Arabic philosophy' suffers from a similar problem: philosophy in the Islamic world has been written in languages other than Arabic, especially Syriac, Hebrew, and Persian.

So then, 'philosophy in the Islamic world'. What should we expect this to include? Well, let's start at the beginning. Islam was born in the 7th century AD (see Box 1) with the revelation given to the Prophet Muḥammad, known as the Qur'ān.

Box 1 The Islamic Calendar

If you are willing to memorize just one date while reading this book, let it be AD 622, which is the year that the Prophet Muḥammad led his followers from his home city of Mecca to settle in Medina. The Muslim calendar is dated from that event, so that you can calculate a year in the Islamic calendar by taking the AD date and subtracting 622. Or you could, if the Islamic calendar were solar. But it is actually a lunar calendar, and lunar years are shorter than solar years. So the further towards the present you go, the less you have to subtract to get the right answer: I'm writing this introduction in August AD 2014, which falls in 1435 AH (a gap of only 579 years). Just as AD stands for *anno domini*, meaning 'year of our Lord', AH stands for *anno hegirae*, referring to the Arabic *ḥijra*, the 'pilgrimage' to Medina. In the rest of this book I'll give only the AD dates, which I assume will be more useful to most readers.

The revelation handed down to Muḥammad insisted on the oneness of God (*tawḥīd*), promised reward for those who believe in and obey Him, and threatened punishment for those who do not. Muḥammad is identified in the Qur'ān as a paradigm to be emulated by other Muslims. For this reason, memories of the Prophet's deeds and sayings were passed down orally from his companions, and eventually written down by religious scholars. Such a report is called a *ḥadīth*. Along with the Qur'ān, *ḥadīth* forms the basis of Islamic religious teaching and also Islamic law.

That's a sketch of the beginnings of Islam itself. What about the beginnings of philosophy under Islam? It's usual to identify the beginning of philosophy in the Islamic world with a translation movement that began more than 200 years after the age of the Prophet. From the end of the 8th century until the beginning of the 10th century, many works of Greek science and philosophy were rendered into Arabic. The most famous philosophers of the Islamic world, namely al-Kindī, al-Fārābī, Avicenna, Averroes, and Maimonides, responded directly to these translations, and especially to the Arabic versions of Aristotle. The tradition they represent was called *falsafa*. As you can tell, this is just an Arabic version of the Greek word *philosophia*, so that the very name of the discipline marked its foreignness. Usually, what people have in mind when they talk about 'philosophy' in the Islamic world is this Hellenizing tradition of *falsafa*.

I however favour a broader understanding, which refuses to ignore material of philosophical interest just because it was not written by so-called 'philosophers (*falāsifa*)'. The historian of philosophy will find intriguing ideas in some commentaries on the Qur'ān (*tafsīr*), in classical works on Arabic grammar, and in treatises on the principles of Islamic law (*fiqh*). But for the purposes of this book, the main traditions that need to be considered alongside *falsafa* are *kalām* and sufism. You will presumably have heard of sufism, the mystical tradition of Islam, and its Jewish counterpart the Kabbalah, some of whose key texts were written in the Islamic world. *Kalām* is a less familiar word. In fact it literally means 'word', but is usually translated as 'theology' or 'rational theology'. The theologians, or *mutakallimūn*, were said to be doing the 'science of the word (*'ilm al-kalām*)', for reasons that remain somewhat obscure. Perhaps it was because they were exploring the meaning of God's word, that is, His revelation. The *mutakallimūn* explored numerous subjects of obvious philosophical importance, for instance proofs of God's existence, human freedom, and even atomistic theories of matter.

An exclusive focus on *falsafa* has often gone hand-in-hand with exclusive focus on a restricted time period, beginning with al-Kindī in the 9th century and ending with Averroes, who died in 1198. Averroes has frequently been seen as the last philosopher of Islam. This is not only because he is the last great representative of Hellenic-inspired *falsafa*. It is also because he and his contemporary Maimonides are the last thinkers from the Islamic world to exercise significant influence on Latin medieval philosophy. Taking a European perspective, historians of philosophy have thus tended to ignore later developments in the Eastern heartlands of the Islamic world, when philosophy was often pursued in the context of *kalām* and sufism. Only recently have scholars begun to explore philosophical developments in the 13th century and beyond. I will duly be sketching those developments in the chronological survey you are about to read. In the thematic sections of the book, I will be alluding to thinkers from across the ages, right down to the 20th century.

Chapter 1
A historical whirlwind tour

Within a few generations of the rise of Islam, the new religion spread across a huge swath of territory, from the Iberian peninsula in the West to the borders of India and China in the East (see Map 1). Most of this territory still belongs to the Islamic world today, and more besides: nowadays Indonesia is the nation with the highest number of Muslims, and Islam is the second most popular religion in India. Naturally, it would be an exaggeration to say that philosophy has flourished in Islamic culture at all places and times. But the widespread idea that philosophy in the Islamic world declined, or even vanished, towards the end of the medieval period is equally false. This misconception is so deeply embedded that philosophy in the Islamic world is most often taught at university level as a part of *medieval* philosophy. Yet the full story goes well past the medieval period and down to the present day.

The formative period

The medieval period of Europe overlaps with most of what I am calling the 'formative period': the time up to Avicenna (d. 1037). Ancient Greek philosophy became known in the Islamic world a couple of centuries before Avicenna, but our story begins earlier, with the arguments that raged among theologians (*mutakallimūn*) in the 8th century. A good place to start would be Wāṣil ibn ʿAṭāʾ (d. 748), who is given credit for founding the *kalām* movement known as the Muʿtazilites. This label is slightly misleading. The early theologians spent much of their energy arguing with one another, and did not yet see themselves as adhering to a standard list of Muʿtazilite doctrines. Still, Wāṣil and several other early thinkers, especially Abū l-Hudhayl (d. 849), did hold views that would later be adopted by thinkers who thought of themselves explicitly as Muʿtazilites.

The Muʿtazilites were styled as 'the upholders of unity (*tawḥīd*) and justice (*ʿadl*)', a phrase which gives us a good way into seeing how their theological doctrines hung together. They were staunch defenders of God's unity—not exactly a controversial stance, given that the core teaching of Islam is monotheism. But they interpreted divine unity in an unusually strict way, rejecting the existence of multiple attributes distinct from God. As for the idea that God is just, the Muʿtazilites again had a controversial interpretation of this uncontroversial claim. They believed that human reason can discern the nature of moral obligation. For instance, we perceive that it would be unjust—even for God—to punish people for deeds they cannot help committing. This led the Muʿtazilites to one of their signature doctrines: the affirmation of human freedom.

Other theologians objected to the Muʿtazilites' confident application of human reason. For these opponents, we should base our beliefs on revelation alone. Some went so far as to accept that God has a body because the Qurʾān speaks of Him as having a face, or as sitting upon a throne. Naturally, the Muʿtazilites too saw revelation as an indispensable source for theology. Those who doubt their credentials as 'philosophers', preferring to reserve this term for thinkers who engaged with the Greek tradition, might point to the fact that the Muʿtazilites did argue on the basis of citations from the Qurʾān and *ḥadīth* (see further Box 2). But of course, the holy texts of Islam were common ground between all the theologians, except for disagreements about which *ḥadīth* should be accepted as

Box 2 The *miḥna*

In 833, the caliph al-Maʾmūn declared his support for a Muʿtazilite doctrine: the createdness of the Qurʾān. This teaching went together with the Muʿtazilite understanding of divine unity. The Qurʾān is the word of God, and thus can be seen as one of His attributes. To accept that this word is eternal rather than created would, according to the Muʿtazilites, make it a second divine entity alongside God Himself. That would violate the core Islamic principle of *tawḥīd* (God's oneness). Al-Maʾmūn and his successors, the very caliphs who sponsored the translation of Greek scientific works into Arabic, imposed an 'inquisition' or 'test' (*miḥna*) in which religious scholars and judges were required to accept that the Qurʾān was created. Some defied the caliphs and were persecuted, most famously Aḥmad ibn Ḥanbal. But in the end the attempt to enforce theological conformity failed. Ibn Ḥanbal was widely admired for his stance; one of the four orthodox legal schools of sunni Islam would come to be named for him. After the *miḥna* political rulers of sunni Islam would generally leave the theological debates to the scholars or *ʿulamāʾ*, a stark contrast to the top-down enforcement of orthodoxy we find in medieval Christendom. Perhaps for this reason, there has rarely been persecution aimed at *philosophical* beliefs in the Islamic world, even when those beliefs were markedly opposed to mainstream religious convictions. By contrast, sectarian *religious* beliefs have often been treated as politically seditious, with shiites persecuted by sunni rulers and vice-versa.

reliable. In an effort to solve interpretive deadlocks, debates within *kalām* often had recourse to rational argumentation.

Another reason to begin our overview before the Greek-Arabic translation movement is that the movement did not occur in a vacuum. Already in late antiquity, Hellenic philosophy

1. Aristotle teaching Alexander the Great, as pictured in a 13th-century Arabic manuscript.

(see Figure 1) found its way into a Semitic language: not Arabic, but Syriac. In a foreshadowing of the ʿAbbāsid-sponsored Greek-Arabic translations, Christian scholars working at monasteries in Syria produced versions of works by Aristotle and other Greek thinkers.

Some Christians, for instance Sergius of Rēsh'aynā (d. 536), composed their own philosophical treatises. This Christian scholarly tradition provided continuity between the Hellenic and Islamic cultures. When Islam spread through the Near East, Greek-speaking Christians fell within its sphere of influence. They retained their religious beliefs, and there continued to be scholars with facility in both Greek and Syriac. So when the 'Abbāsid caliphs and other wealthy patrons of the 8th–10th centuries decided to have Greek scientific works rendered into Arabic, most of the translators they hired were Christians. This activity was centred in Iraq and particularly Baghdad, the new capital city founded by the early 'Abbasid caliph al-Manṣūr.

One outstanding translation group was gathered around the Christian medical expert Ḥunayn ibn Isḥāq (d. 873). He specialized in translating the works of Galen, the greatest doctor of late antiquity. His son, the somewhat confusingly named Isḥāq ibn Ḥunayn (d. 910/11; 'Ibn' means 'son', so his name simply means 'Isḥāq son of Ḥunayn'), concentrated on Aristotelian philosophy. Philosophy was also the focus of another group, the 'Kindī circle'. Their leader was al-Kindī (d. after 870), the first *faylasūf* of Islam, that is, the first to engage with the newly translated Greek scientific and philosophical works. He does not seem to have known Greek himself, and he was a Muslim, yet he coordinated the efforts of a group of Christian translators. In addition to versions of treatises by Aristotle, the Kindī circle also produced Arabic translations of works by the two greatest late ancient Platonists, Plotinus (d. 270) and Proclus (d. 485). Probably due to a misunderstanding of prefatory comments that were added to the text in the Kindī circle, parts of the Arabic version of Plotinus were transmitted as the *Theology of Aristotle*. In other words, a major work of ancient Platonism was thought to be by Aristotle himself. A similar confusion attached to the Arabic Proclus. A version of the Kindī circle translation of Proclus' *Elements of Theology* became known in Latin Christendom as the *Book of Causes* (*Liber de Causis*), also ascribed to Aristotle.

Al-Kindī was deeply influenced by these Neoplatonic sources, and by the genuine Aristotle, as well as a wide range of other translated sources. He was particularly interested in mathematical works by authors like Euclid and Ptolemy. He drew these ideas together in a series of treatises, often in the form of epistles addressed to his patrons, who included the ʿAbbāsid caliph al-Muʿtaṣim and the caliph's son, whom al-Kindī tutored. These treatises set out to prove the agreement between Islam and Greek philosophy, in order to display the value of the newly translated materials for the educated elite of al-Kindī's day. In his most important work, *On First Philosophy*, al-Kindī used Greek ideas to portray God's unity in a way reminiscent of the Muʿtazilites, and to prove that the created universe is not eternal. But al-Kindī did not restrict his attention to theological questions. He wrote on a bewildering range of topics, from cosmology to ethics to the soul, to more practical topics like swords and perfumes. There are often connections between al-Kindī's philosophy and his contributions in the applied disciplines. His epistles on cosmology provided an implicit rationale for other treatises on astrology, and his Pythagorean interests in mathematics played a role in several writings on music and even in a work on pharmacology.

We can trace his influence among a number of thinkers who form a 'Kindian tradition'. These figures, who included first-, second- and third-generation students of al-Kindī, followed his lead in seeing harmony between Islam and Greek philosophy, especially the Platonism they found in the Arabic versions of Plotinus and Proclus. The most important representatives of this tradition were al-ʿĀmirī (d. 991), author of (among other things) a reworking of the Arabic Proclus materials, and Miskawayh (d. 1030), who quoted al-Kindī at the end of his influential ethical treatise *The Refinement of Character*. Thinkers of the Kindian tradition, like al-Kindī himself, tended to be all-round intellectuals and not just philosophers. Throughout the formative period, philosophy was frequently pursued as just one among several cultivated arts

2. Portrait of the 10th-century Platonists known as the Brethren of Purity.

among the intelligentsia (see Figure 2). Miskawayh, for instance, is well known for his work as a historian.

But philosophy also had its detractors. In a famous debate at the court of a Baghdad vizier, a Christian philosopher and exponent of the quintessential Hellenic discipline of logic, Abū Bishr Mattā (d. 940), was publicly embarrassed by a grammarian, al-Sīrāfī (d. 979). Abū Bishr lost the battle, but not the war. Eventually logic would be widely adopted by Muslim theologians. In the shorter term, a group of Aristotelian philosophers associated with Abū Bishr would flourish for several generations. Mostly this group, the 'Baghdad Peripatetics', were Christians who devoted their attention to commenting on Aristotle, with forays into Trinitarian theology and Biblical exegesis. The most outstanding Christian member of the school was Yaḥyā ibn ʿAdī, from whom we have a number of philosophical and theological treatises. But a more famous name belongs to a Muslim connected to the group: al-Fārābī (d. 950). He shared his Christian colleagues' interest in logic, and likewise wrote commentaries on Aristotle. His fame is, however, due more to his original systematic works, which integrate Aristotelian philosophy with themes from Neoplatonism. Against this cosmological and metaphysical setting, he set out an innovative political philosophy, influential on later thinkers like Averroes and Naṣīr al-Dīn al-Ṭūsī.

Jews as well as Christians played a major role in the philosophy of the formative period. We have a polite philosophical correspondence between Yaḥyā ibn ʿAdī and a Jewish philosopher, and al-Kindī's writings were used extensively by one of the earliest Jewish thinkers in the Islamic world, Isaac Israeli (d. *c.*907). Jews also adopted ideas from the Islamic theology of their day. The chief example is Saadia Gaon (d. 942), a formidable scholar who wrote on Jewish law and Hebrew grammar, translated the Bible into Arabic, and composed a major philosophical-theological work, the *Book of Doctrines and Beliefs*. He has much in common with al-Kindī, for instance in his discussion of the eternity of the universe. But Saadia is most often compared to the Muʿtazilites, whose positions on human freedom and divine attributes he echoed and further developed.

Box 3 Al-Rāzī *vs* the Ismāʿīlīs

The works translated in the Kindī circle were popular among not just sunni Muslims, but also among shiites, and particularly the group of shiites called the Ismāʿīlīs. Shiite Muslims believe that legitimate rule over the Muslim community should have passed directly from the Prophet Muḥammad to his cousin and son-in-law ʿAlī, and then to ʿAlī's line of male descendants—with different branches of shiite Muslims accepting different descendants as the legitimate leaders of the faith, or imams. Some Ismāʿīlī missionaries used Platonist concepts to explain the special insight granted to the imam. They were challenged by sunni Muslims, including a man with a very idiosyncratic approach to philosophy and religion: Abū Bakr al-Rāzī (d. 925). One of the greatest doctors of Islam, al-Rāzī developed his philosophy under the inspiration of the ancient medical writer Galen rather than Aristotle. His resulting theory of five 'eternal principles' was set out in works that are now lost, but we have reports about it from his greatest intellectual opponents, the Ismāʿīlīs. They portrayed him as an irreverent heretic, who denied the validity of all prophecy. He responded to one such critic by accusing the Ismāʿīlīs of slavish devotion to authority (*taqlīd*).

Avicenna

In the wake of the translation movement, then, philosophy was developing in different ways among thinkers of various faiths. There was the hard-core Aristotelianism of the Baghdad school, the more irenic and broadminded stance of the Kindian tradition, anti-philosophical criticism from men like al-Sīrāfī, and jostling for supremacy between Hellenic-inspired philosophy and Islamic *kalām*. But the situation would change in the 11th century, thanks to a thinker from the central Asian city of Bukhārā whose impact was unparalleled: Abū ʿAlī ibn Sīnā, usually known in English by his Latinized name Avicenna (d. 1037). As we can see from a brief intellectual autobiography composed by Avicenna, he was a confident and largely self-taught genius who reserved the right to pass judgement on all his philosophical predecessors. In a series of works covering all the departments of philosophy, above all his magisterial *Healing* (*al-Shifāʾ*), Avicenna thoroughly reworked the ideas of the Aristotelian tradition as it had come down to him.

After Avicenna, philosophers had a stark choice: take Avicenna as the new starting-point, or try to undo the damage by retrieving the authentically Hellenic legacy. In the Eastern heartlands of Islam, the latter was attempted by ʿAbd al-Laṭīf al-Baghdādī (d. 1231), who despised Avicenna and tried to go back to Aristotle. But in these regions nearly everyone chose the former approach of engaging with Avicenna. Sometimes the engagement was highly critical, most famously in the case of al-Ghazālī (d. 1111), whose *Incoherence of the Philosophers* took aim at Avicenna rather than Aristotle. Over the longer term, theologians in the East would continue to criticize, but also selectively borrow from, Avicenna's philosophy. The result was a long-lived tradition of *kalām* shot through with his distinctive terminology and distinctions. Out in the Muslim province of al-Andalus (modern-day Spain and Portugal), the situation was rather different.

Andalusia

Already the early Andalusian jurist Ibn Ḥazm (d. 1063) was able to study with a representative of the Aristotelian Baghdad school. This is the brand of philosophy that for the most part won out in Andalusia. Avicenna was much admired by Ibn Ṭufayl (d. 1185), author of the philosophical novel *Ḥayy ibn Yaqẓān*, in which the title character grows up alone on a desert island and becomes a self-taught philosopher. But even Ibn Ṭufayl complained of having poor access to Avicenna's works. His predecessor, Ibn Bājja (Avempace, d. 1139), was much more influenced by Aristotle and by al-Fārābī, who exerted great influence on both Muslim and

Jewish thinkers in Andalusia. Those who drew on al-Fārābī included the greatest Aristotelian exegete of the Islamic world: Ibn Rushd, like Avicenna usually known by a Latinized version of his name, Averroes (d. 1198). He produced numerous commentaries on the works of Aristotle in different formats. In them Averroes shows his mastery of both the Aristotelian texts and his commentators, from late antiquity to al-Fārābī and Ibn Bājja.

Averroes was not particularly influential among Muslim thinkers, for whom his revival of the Baghdad school's Aristotle-centred philosophical project was no longer relevant. But in Latin Christendom, where the works of Aristotle were just attracting renewed interest in the 12th and 13th centuries, Averroes became the chief guide. Aristotle was called simply 'the Philosopher', and Averroes 'the Commentator'. Averroes' influence was perhaps even greater among Jewish readers in Andalusia and beyond: among readers of Hebrew it became common to consult Averroes' commentaries and summaries of Aristotle rather than Aristotle himself. The great Jewish commentator Levi Ben Gerson (Gersonides, d. 1344) devoted his exegetical works to the exegeses of Averroes, producing 'super-commentaries' on the latter's commentaries.

That was in the 14th century, by which point Jewish philosophy in Andalusia had been a going concern for quite some time. Already in the 11th century, we have Solomon ibn Gabirol (Avicebron, d. 1057/8) and his philosophical treatise *The Fountain of Life* (known often by its Latin title, *Fons Vitae*). This is not an overtly Jewish work, but rather a treatise drawing on Neoplatonic sources to articulate the relationship between God and created things. Ibn Gabirol also wove philosophical themes into his poems, which were a highpoint of Jewish literature in Andalusia. His *Fountain of Life* was written in Arabic, but the poems in Hebrew—setting an example for generations to follow, who often wrote philosophy in Arabic or Judeo-Arabic (written in Hebrew letters), whereas poetry and works on Jewish law or biblical commentary were typically in Hebrew. We see this in the greatest Jewish thinker of the medieval age, and arguably of all time: Maimonides (d. 1204), who wrote legal treatises in Hebrew but philosophy in Arabic.

When it came to philosophy, Maimonides adopted the Aristotelian project inherited from al-Fārābī, like his contemporary Averroes. He sought to reconcile this project with the Jewish tradition, clearing up apparent conflicts between the two in his famous *Guide for the Perplexed.* For some later Jewish thinkers, the *Guide* was unsettling in its rationalism and devotion to the Aristotelian tradition. Copies of the work were, infamously, burnt by Christian authorities in southern France in the 1230s. This occurred at the behest of Jewish conservatives who were alarmed by the rationalism of Maimonides and his supporters—for instance Samuel ibn Tibbon (d. 1230), who translated the *Guide* into Hebrew. The so-called 'Maimonides controversy' reflected the deep disagreement among Jews about the value of doing philosophy. But even the opponents of rationalist Maimonideanism acknowledged the authority of Maimonides himself when it came to questions of Jewish law.

The development of philosophy in Andalusia stands as the peak of Jewish thought in the medieval period, with Maimonides as the apex of that peak. This was possible because of the favourable conditions enjoyed by Jews in Muslim culture—a general feature of Islamic society throughout the medieval period, but particularly marked in Andalusia. Scholars frequently speak of the *convivencia*, the 'living together' of Jews, Muslims, and also Christians on the Iberian peninsula. This came to an end during Maimonides' lifetime, with the invasion of the fundamentalist Almohads. Maimonides fled with his family and wound up living and working in Cairo, while other Jews relocated to Christian realms, including southern France. After the Christian 'reconquest' of Andalusia, the situation improved, but there was an appalling pogrom in 1391, when the Jews of Barcelona and elsewhere were massacred. One of the victims was the son of Ḥasdai Crescas (d. 1410/11), a brilliant philosopher and critic of Maimonidean Aristotelianism. Almost exactly a century later, the story of Muslim and Jewish thought in Andalusia would come to an end, when the last Jews and Muslims were exiled in 1492.

Box 4 Mysticism in Andalusia

For the subsequent history of philosophy in the Islamic world, the most influential thinker from Andalusia was Ibn ʿArabī (d. 1240), born in Mercia though he later relocated to Damascus. He drew together themes espoused by earlier figures, like the great female mystic Rābiʿa (d. 790s) and the provocative sufi martyr al-Ḥallāj (d. 922). For Ibn ʿArabī and other sufis, God lay beyond the grasp of human reason. Yet He shows Himself to us in the form of the universe He has created and in the revelation, especially the names He has given to Himself in the Qurʾān. Ibn ʿArabī set the stage for the later development of philosophical sufism, perpetuated in Andalusia by Ibn Sabʿīn (d. 1270) and in Anatolia by al-Qūnawī (d. 1274), who integrated Ibn ʿArabī's ideas with Avicennan philosophy at the same time as al-Qūnawī's friend Rūmī (d. 1273) was writing his famous mystical poems in the Persian language. Mysticism also blossomed among Jews in Andalusia, with the emergence of the *Kabbalah*, meaning 'tradition'. Kabbalistic authors took inspiration from several late antique texts that adopted a symbolic approach to the divine—for instance by assigning numerical values to the limbs of God's body. (A vivid contrast with the rationalism of Maimonides, who declared it the duty of all Jews to believe in God's incorporeality!) One medieval text of the Kabbalah, the *Zohar*, in fact presents itself as a late antique work. Much as the sufis sought to grasp God insofar as possible through His names, the medieval Kabbalists spoke of ten *sefirot* (roughly, 'numbers') through which God shows Himself to His creation, while Himself remaining utterly transcendent.

Reactions to Avicenna

In the East, Avicenna supplanted Aristotle as *the* philosopher, but he attracted as many critics as admirers. Aside from al-Ghazālī, the most famous critic was Suhrawardī (d. 1191), founder of what he styled as a new 'Illuminationist' (*ishrāqī*) tradition of philosophy. Like sufis who were inspired by Ibn ʿArabī (see Figure 3 and Box 4), Suhrawardī wove together ideas from the philosophical tradition with mystical themes. But Suhrawardī's taste was rather exotic when it came to his inspirations. In his greatest work, *The Philosophy of Illumination* (*Ḥikmat al-Ishrāq*), he claimed solidarity with ancient sages like Plato, for instance by affirming the reality of Platonic Forms. In fact Suhrawardī presented his Illuminationism as a recovery of the wisdom of several civilizations: Greek, Persian, and Indian. At the core of this Illuminationist philosophy, as the name suggests, was the concept of light. God, the 'Light of lights', creates by spreading forth rays of illumination that become progressively dimmer, with bodies constituting 'dark' obstacles to the divine splendour. All this was put forward in opposition to what Suhrwardī called the 'Peripetatic' philosophy, which for him meant Avicennism, not Aristotelianism.

Alongside Suhrawardī and a few thinkers in the subsequent generations who commented on his works (especially al-Shahrazūrī, d. after 1288), another line of response to Avicenna developed within the Ashʿarite school of *kalām*. This school's founder, al-Ashʿarī (d. 935/36), began as an adherent of the Muʿtazilite doctrines but came to reject them. Against the Muʿtazilites' austere conception of divine unity, the Ashʿarites accepted the distinct reality of God's attributes. They also believed that the Muʿtazilite stance on human freedom was insufficient to safeguard God's omnipotence, and insisted that God creates absolutely everything other than Himself, including human actions. If the core of Muʿtazilism was its faith in the power of human reason,

3. The tomb of Ibn ʿArabi in Syria.

the core of Ash'arism was respect for God's untrammelled power and freedom to do as He sees fit. Even moral obligations, from their point of view, arise only once God has laid them upon His creatures. Hence the Ash'arites endorsed a 'divine command' theory of morality, whereas the Mu'tazilites thought that even God must adhere to certain moral principles.

Though Mu'tazilism did live on in the post-formative period, the Ash'arites (and a similar school, the Māturīdīs) became the dominant force in sunni theology. Avicenna seems to have been influenced by Ash'arism to some extent, though to what extent is a matter of debate. There's no debating the influence in the other direction, as Ash'arite theology absorbed Avicenna's thought. Even the assault on Avicenna in al-Ghazālī's *Incoherence* falls short of a thorough rejection. After all, he refutes only certain Avicennan theses, implying that the others may be acceptable. (A similar range of Avicennan theses was targeted slightly later by another Ash'arite, al-Shahrastānī (d. 1153).) Furthermore, al-Ghazālī insists on the value of disciplines like logic and astronomy, dismissing critics of the latter by quoting the proverb, 'a rational foe is better than an ignorant friend'. So it was arguably in part thanks to, rather than in spite of, al-Ghazālī that Avicennan philosophy and especially Avicennan logic became abiding interests of later Ash'arites.

A particularly outstanding representative of philosophical Ash'arism was Fakhr al-Dīn al-Rāzī (d. 1210), who is not to be confused with the above-mentioned Abū Bakr al-Rāzī (the name 'al-Rāzī' just means someone from the Persian city of Rayy). Fakhr al-Dīn wrote lengthy and complex treatises covering many of the main topics raised by Avicenna's philosophy, enumerating arguments for and against a range of possible views on each topic. Fakhr al-Dīn was an appreciative exegete of Avicenna as well as a critic. Evidence for this is his detailed, though often critical, commentary on Avicenna's late work *Pointers and Reminders* (*al-Ishārāt wa-l-tanbīhāt*). This commentary provoked a backlash from the greatest Avicennan of the 13th century, Naṣīr al-Dīn al-Ṭūsī, who wrote a counter-commentary on the *Pointers* that is far more approving of Avicenna's arguments. Yet al-Ṭūsī was not just a commentator, a kind of second Averroes devoted to Avicenna rather than Aristotle. To the contrary, he was a protean thinker, who at different stages of his career espoused two varieties of shiite Islam, and who could sound either mystical or highly rationalist depending on context.

Furthermore, al-Ṭūsī made great contributions in the sciences, especially astronomy. He was the head of a group of philosophers and scholars at an astronomical observatory sited at Marāgha in modern-day Azerbaijan (see Figure 4). This group's members were remarkably varied in philosophical approach, though all had an interest in some core disciplines like logic and of course astronomy. They included a major Illuminationist thinker, Quṭb al-Dīn al-Shīrāzī (d. 1311), an Avicennan theologian named al-Kātibī (d. 1276), who rethought Avicenna's logic in one of the most widely read logical textbooks of all time, *al-Risāla al-Shamsiyya*, and even a Christian philosopher, Bar Hebraeus (d. 1286). To complete the ecumenical picture, we can add that al-Ṭūsī exchanged philosophical views with Ibn Kammūna, a Jewish thinker who took an interest in Suhrawardī's Illuminationist philosophy. Nor was Ibn Kammūna the first Jewish author involved in this long-running engagement with Avicenna. Earlier, a Jewish-Muslim convert named Abū l-Barākāt al-Baghdādī (d. 1160s) had written the *Book of What Has Been Carefully Considered* (*Kitāb al-Muʿtabar*). As the title suggests, Abū l-Barākāt was passing judgement on previous philosophers, including Avicenna, in much the way that Avicenna had passed judgement on the Aristotelian tradition. In the process, Abū l-Barākāt made some proposals on topics in physics not unlike those of the aforementioned (but chronologically later) Western Jewish critic of Maimonides, Ḥasdai Crescas.

4. A 15th-century Persian manuscript of Naṣīr al-Dīn al-Ṭūsī's observatory at Maragha depicting astronomers at work teaching astronomy, including how to use an astrolabe. The instrument hangs on the observatory's wall.

The Mongol period

With al-Ṭūsī's group at the Marāgha observatory, we already reach the time of the Mongol invasions, which spread death, destruction, and disruption across the Eastern Islamic lands. Surprisingly, philosophy and scientific activity were able to survive and even find sponsorship under the Mongols. The Marāgha observatory enjoyed the patronage of Hülegü, the Mongol conqueror of Baghdad (according to legend, al-Ṭūsī advised him on how to execute the last ʿAbbāsid caliph). A later ruler of Mongol descent, Ulegh Beg, sponsored another observatory at Samarqand. The royal court of Samarqand could also boast of significant intellectuals, for instance the theologian al-Taftazānī (d. 1390). He and earlier Mongol-era sunni theologians like al-Ījī (d. 1355) produced comprehensive summaries of the philosophically tinged sunni *kalām* pioneered in the previous couple of centuries. These duly became the object of further commentaries, and were studied by many generations of young religious scholars in *madrasas* across the Islamic world. In fact works by theologians, together with standard commentaries, were still being studied at al-Azhar university in Cairo in the 20th century, as were logical treatises like the aforementioned *Risāla al-Shamsiyya* of al-Kātibī. In the formative period intellectuals like al-Kindī and al-Fārābī expected philosophy to supplant *kalām*, using the tools of Hellenic wisdom to provide superior answers to questions raised by the Islamic revelation. In the end, something very different happened. *Kalām* became a vehicle for the spread of philosophy, albeit that the philosophy in question derived from Avicenna rather than Aristotle or Plotinus.

These developments were remarked upon by some of the sharper observers of the time. No observer was sharper than the historian Ibn Khaldūn (d. 1406), who had the luxury of witnessing the Mongol invasion from a safe distance, since he came from the Western Islamic world (the 'maghreb'). He noted that Hellenic philosophy had been replaced by something new—'as if the books of the ancients had never been'—and that *kalām* and philosophy had become effectively indistinguishable. Ibn Khaldūn himself stood outside of that tradition. Neither an Avicennan nor a *mutakallim*, he innovatively applied the empirical lessons of Aristotelian science to the subject of human history. Looking back over the rise of Islam and the success of tribal groups like the Almohads in Andalusia, Ibn Khaldūn came to a general theory about the rise and fall of political dynasties.

Similar observations about fusion of philosophy with *kalām* had already been made earlier, with no little alarm, by Ibn Taymiyya (d. 1328). He promoted a radical approach to jurisprudence (see Box 5), which rejected centuries' worth of legal orthodoxy in favour of what he perceived as the teachings of the first Muslim generations. Ibn Taymiyya also railed against the various corruptions

Box 5 The Islamic legal schools

There is a long history of mutual interaction between law and philosophy in the Islamic world. It was common for both Jewish and Muslim philosophers to be legal scholars: al-Ghazālī, Averroes, and Maimonides are only the most famous examples. Within Islam, there are four orthodox legal *madhhabs* or schools in sunni Islam, each named after an esteemed religious authority: the Ḥanafīs, the Ḥanbalīs, the Shāfiʿīs, and the Mālikīs. They largely agreed on broad methodological issues, but were distinguished by areas of geographical dominance (for instance the Mālikīs were the main school in the West) and on many points of legal detail. In addition the shiite Muslims had their own legal tradition. Within sunni Islam there were other, less influential approaches to law. For instance the Andalusian jurist Ibn Ḥazm was a Ẓāhirī, meaning that he followed only the 'evident (*ẓāhir*)' meaning of pronouncements in the Qurʾān and *ḥadīth*, without drawing analogies or inferences as did the jurists of the orthodox schools.

he perceived in Muslim intellectual life. Unlike the earlier critic of philosophy al-Ghazālī, Ibn Taymiyya had nothing but scorn for the discipline of logic. He wrote at length about its uselessness, remarking that expertise in logic is like camel meat on a mountain top: hard to reach, and not worth much once you've got it. Nor was he impressed by 'philosophical sufis' (his phrase), who to his mind represented as grave a threat to Islam as the Mongol hordes.

Three empires

By the beginning of the 16th century, the chaos caused by the Mongols was fading into memory and new political realities were settling in. Three powerful empires controlled most of the Islamic world (see Map 3). The earliest to rise to dominance were the Ottomans, who managed to take Constantinople from the Byzantines in 1453. Somewhat later, in India, rulers with Mongol blood-lines founded the Mughal dynasty. Under both Ottomans and Mughals, philosophy continued along more or less the lines we have seen in the Mongol period. The 'intellectual sciences' were practised in both empires. Sophisticated astronomical work was done in the Ottoman realm by figures like 'Alā' al-Dīn al-Qūshjī (d. 1474). In Mughal India, a standard curriculum developed for the study of philosophical *kalām*, the so-called *dars-i niẓāmī*, named for Niẓām al-Dīn Sihālavī (d. 1748), a scholar who helped determine which works should be studied. He was a member of a family of scholars, the Farangī Maḥall, who emerged in Lucknow in the 18th century. In the 19th century another family, the Khayrabādīs, would carry on the practice of study and commentary on the classical works of Avicennizing *kalām*.

A similar programme of study was followed under the Ottomans, though Kātib Çelebi (d. 1657) worried that the intellectual sciences were stagnating in his day. Philosophical *kalām* had competition from other intellectual currents. For the moderate Çelebi, one worry was a populist religious movement, the Kādīzādelis, strong critics of corruption among the scholarly class or *ʿulamāʾ*. Like Ibn Taymiyya before them, the Kādīzādelis also took aim at the excesses of sufis. But philosophical sufism continued to thrive in the face of such criticisms. In India, a Mughal prince named Dārā Shikūh (d. 1659) even wrote about the harmony between sufism and the teachings of classical India. A later mystical philosopher of India, Shāh Walī Allāh (d. 1762), was also convinced that multiple religions could represent versions of the single eternal truth. Through it all, the *madrasas* of both empires continued to teach students logic, and theologians continued to debate the merits of Avicennan philosophy. Earlier in the Ottoman empire, a sultan even asked two scholars to offer competing assessments of al-Ghazālī's criticism of Avicenna in the *Incoherence of the Philosophers*.

All of which should make it clear that philosophy and science did not, as is so often supposed, vanish in the Islamic world after the medieval period. And we haven't even mentioned the best known of the later philosophical traditions, which unfolded in Persia. In the early 16th century, the area corresponding to modern-day Iran fell under the sway of the shiite Safavid dynasty. Just before and during the rise of the Safavids, three significant thinkers emerged in the Persian city of Shīrāz: Jalāl al-Dīn al-Dawānī (d. 1501), Ṣadr al-Dīn al-Dashtakī (d. 1498), and the latter's son Ghiyāth al-Dīn al-Dashtakī (d. 1541). A hostile rivalry between the two Dashtakīs and Dawānī was fought out over questions of logic, metaphysics, and the interpretation of Avicenna. Their mutual refutations, often presented in commentaries or glosses on earlier thinkers, would themselves be made the object of many commentaries in the coming centuries (see Figure 5).

But the greatest thinker of early modern Iran is universally acknowledged to be Mullā Ṣadrā (d. 1640). He typified the syncretic tendencies of philosophy under the Safavids. Like the earlier Ismāʿīlī thinkers (see Box 3), Safavid philosophers found Hellenic Platonism to be a good fit with shiite theology, and Greek-Arabic philosophical translations were thus read with the

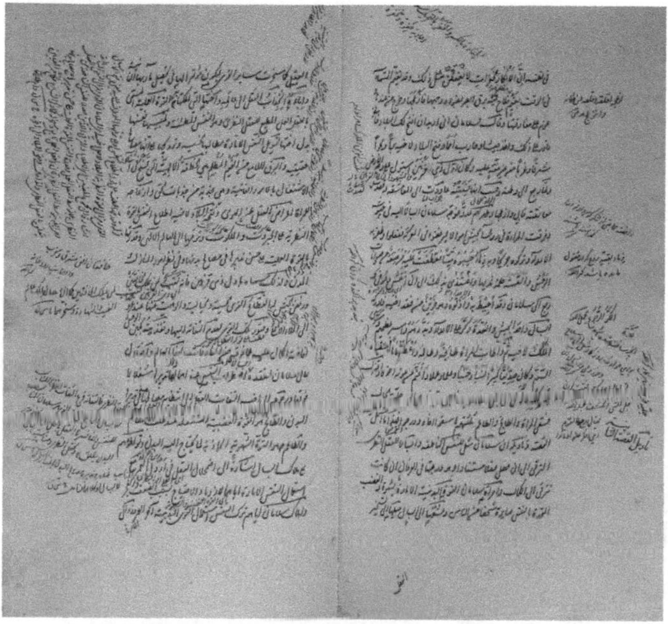

5. Manuscript image showing how glosses were added to comment on philosophical texts.

sort of careful attention they had rarely received since Avicenna. We even find commentaries being written on the Arabic Plotinus, or *Theology of Aristotle*, at this time. Alongside these Hellenic ideas, Ṣadrā drew on materials from Avicenna, Avicennan *kalām*, and philosophical sufism. Yet he was also a startlingly original thinker, whose theory of 'modulation' in being and substantial change promised to resolve long-standing disputes about existence and the nature of God.

The modern age

Ṣadrā's theories have also met with opposition in some quarters, and though he was always read he became the central inspiration for Iranian philosophy only from the 19th century onwards. This was in part thanks to sympathetic exegesis by Sabzawārī (d. 1878) and more recently 'Allāmah Ṭabāṭabā'ī (d. 1981). Seyyed Hossein Nasr (born 1933), originally from Iran but now an academic based in the United States, has been inspired by Ṣadrā and also by Ṭabāṭabā'ī; the two read philosophy together in Iran. Nasr has also urged a broad, multi-faith and multi-cultural perspective that finds commonalities in many traditions within and beyond the borders of Islam. Taking a page from the book of Shāh Walī Allāh, Nasr sees fundamental agreement between a number of religious traditions on a core set of commitments he calls the 'perennial philosophy'. He has even suggested that these shared values could provide an effective basis for environmentalism, since the perennial philosophy urges the subordination of selfish desire to the good of the whole creation.

While Ṣadrā and other figures from Islamic history have provided inspiration for latter-day intellectuals, philosophical and scientific ideas from beyond the Islamic world have also had an impact. In the 18th century, Ottoman thinkers like the philosophical sufi 'Abd al-Ghanī al-Nābulusī (d. 1731) were already arguing for a 'renewal' of Islam that would respond positively to European science. By the 19th century, the Ottoman sultans were looking to European models as they brought in bureaucratic, military, and educational reforms. This helped launch more radical reform movements, the Young Ottomans and Young Turks, who made frequent mention of European philosophy in formulating their political views. Two leading Young Turks, Ziya Gökalp (d. 1924) and Abdullah Cevdet (d. 1932), drew respectively on the sociology of Émile Durkheim and the theories of Ludwig Büchner and Auguste Comte.

The same point is illustrated by the greatest Muslim political philosopher of the early 20th century, Muḥammad Iqbāl (d. 1938). Iqbāl's political activities in his native India were inspired by the education he received in Europe, and by ideas taken from Friedrich Nietzsche. Islamic intellectual history has in a sense come full circle. Ideas from European philosophers from Descartes to Heidegger have provoked reactions similar to those that greeted the medieval Greek–Arabic translation movement: outright opposition in some quarters, enthusiastic embrace in others, but most often a circumspect approach of reinterpretation and rethinking in light of the Islamic revelation.

Chapter 2
Reason and revelation

The three Abrahamic religions, Judaism, Christianity, and Islam, agree in recognizing a single God who is the source for the existence of all other things, and who has revealed His will to us through a line of prophets. But how should we understand God as a being transcendent beyond all others? What is the nature of the causality He exercised in creating the universe? How does the knowledge granted to the prophet relate to the sort of knowledge available to other humans? If the prophet is also the leader of a community, how does his religious authority relate to his political authority? These questions will all be examined later in this book. First, we're going to look at a more basic issue: how should one go about answering them?

It is easy to assume that intellectuals of all three faiths faced a simple choice. They could either use unaided human reason, or they could turn to revelation, as found in the Hebrew Bible, the New Testament, and the Qur'ān. This is a natural assumption for us to make, since we are nowadays quick to to see an antithesis between science and religion, between reason and faith. Also, we might also expect the situation in the Islamic world to mirror the situation in Latin Christendom. Medieval Christian thinkers like Aquinas clearly distinguished between theology, which draws on revelation, and philosophy, which uses only the natural light of reason. Something like this distinction was embodied in the very structure of Latin medieval education, with the 'arts' faculty being distinct from the theology faculty in the newly risen universities.

But we should try to free ourselves of these assumptions in approaching the Islamic world. It is unhelpful to see the rivalry, and ultimate reconciliation, between *kalām* and *falsafa* as a confrontation between 'faith' and 'reason'. Rather, there was a struggle within *kalām* itself between more and less rationalist approaches to understanding the revelation brought by Muḥammad. Nor should critics of philosophy be indiscriminately tarred with the brush of 'anti-rationalism'. Al-Ghazālī criticized Avicenna not for doing philosophy, but for making mistakes in his philosophy ('reckless precipitance of the philosophers' would be a more literal translation of the title of his *Tahāfut al-Falāsifa* than 'incoherence of the philosophers'). Ibn Taymiyya insisted that reason (*'aql*) is in full agreement with the Qur'ānic revelation, though his understanding of 'reason' was not the same as that of the philosophers. Other, more mystically inclined authors pointed to the limitations of reason. Yet they often granted, even emphasized, that rational argument was effective within its proper boundaries.

The standards of reasoning

Deciding what can, and cannot, be achieved using human reason presupposes an understanding of rationality itself. For authors drawing on the Greek tradition, such an understanding was readily available in the form of Aristotelian logic. Treatises from Aristotle's logical corpus, or *Organon* (see Box 6), were among the first Greek works translated into Arabic. They were immediately put to use, sometimes in surprising contexts. Al-Kindī, for instance, deployed ideas from Aristotle's *Categories* to prove the immateriality of the soul and to refute the Christian doctrine of the Trinity. (A couple of generations later, the Christian logician Yaḥyā ibn 'Adī wrote a counter-refutation.) Adherents of *falsafa*

Box 6 The *Organon*

The ancients referred to a group of nine Aristotelian logical treatises as the *Organon*, or 'instrument', in keeping with their understanding of logic as the indispensable instrument for doing philosophy. The first text in the series was actually not by Aristotle: an *Introduction* (*Eisagoge*) to logic by the late ancient Platonist Porphyry (d. *c*.305), a student of Plotinus. Students of philosophy would start with this, and then go through the following works of Aristotle: *Categories*, *On Interpretation*, *Prior Analytics*, *Posterior Analytics*, *Topics*, *Sophistical Refutations*, *Rhetoric*, *Poetics*.

As a list of works on 'logic', this is rather surprising. Really only the *Prior Analytics* looks more or less like logic as we would imagine it, as Aristotle there set out the types of valid argument and how they relate to one another. (After Avicenna's pioneering work on logic, this also became the main focus of attention among logicians in the Islamic world.) Its sequel, the *Posterior Analytics*, is something more like a treatise on epistemology or philosophy of science. It delineates the requirements that have to be satisfied in order for us to take something as scientifically demonstrated. The *Topics* deals with dialectical debate, and was translated into Arabic very early, perhaps for use in religious disputation. As the title suggests, the *Sophistical Refutations* helps the reader to diagnose bad arguments. As for the *Rhetoric* and *Poetics*, they may seem to us to have nothing at all to do with logic. But great effort was made to fit them into a unified *Organon*, for instance by portraying poetic metaphors as implicit syllogisms.

were distinguished by nothing so much as their interest and expertise in logic.

The logical discipline was thus a tempting target for those who resented the spread of Greek ideas into Arabic-speaking culture.

We see this with the debate between the Christian philosopher Abū Bishr Mattā and the grammarian al-Sīrāfī. Our information about this event, which occurred in 937/8, is indirect and preserved by reporters sympathetic to al-Sīrāfī. But it seems that the logician was indeed trounced by the grammarian. Abū Bishr apparently provoked the debate with the grand claims he made for logic. Quoting Greek commentators on Aristotle, he declared it the indispensable tool for 'knowing correct from faulty speech, and unsound from sound concept (*ma'nā*)'. This claim is likely to find our sympathy. How can one distinguish true from false without understanding the difference between valid and invalid arguments, which is surely the province of logic?

But Abū Bishr went further. He insisted that, whereas grammar operates with the linguistic 'expression' or 'utterance' (*lafẓ*), logic's domain is the level of the mental concept (*ma'nā*) underlying the linguistic expression. Here his Aristotelianism was showing. The idea that language expresses a mental concept can be found at the beginning of Aristotle's *On Interpretation*. There Aristotle adds that different people express the same 'affections of the soul' using different sounds—as when a German says '*Hund*' where an English-speaker would say 'dog'. Logic, inferred Abū Bishr and other members of the Baghdad school, is a universal science that studies the standards of correct reasoning for all humankind. By contrast grammar is parochial, the study of correct *expression* within some given language. Against this, al-Sīrāfī made the powerful point that an intimate knowledge of language is needed to avoid error when we are reasoning. One must be aware of the ambiguous meanings of terms and master grammatical constructions in order to phrase one's thoughts accurately.

Tellingly, he also challenged Abū Bishr to use 'his logic' to solve a hypothetical legal issue about land ownership. This would not be the last time that the reasoning involved in jurisprudence (*fiqh*) would appear as a rival to the theory of reasoning put forward by experts in logic. About four centuries later, Ibn Taymiyya wrote a massive polemic with the self-explanatory title *Refutation of the Logicians*. Like al-Sīrāfī, he pointed to the gulf between real-life reasoning and the idealized syllogisms studied in logic. For instance the number of premises required in a given argument depends, not on rules laid down by Aristotle, but on each person's background knowledge and assumptions. Ibn Taymiyya illustrated with a legal example: if a Muslim who knows that wine is intoxicating hears that the Prophet forbids drinking intoxicating beverages, he will thereby understand that he shouldn't drink wine. Someone who doesn't know that wine is intoxicating would have to add this as an additional premise. But even this premise would leave the argument ineffectual for non-Muslims.

More generally, Ibn Taymiyya argued that the sort of reasoning used in law is more feasible and effective than the sort fetishized by the philosophers. Aristotle and his followers had understood knowledge in the strict and proper sense (Greek *episteme*, Arabic *ʿilm*) as involving necessary and universal truth claims, in which one general term is predicated of another. So a standard scientific syllogism for the Aristotelians would be something like this:

All giraffes are animals
All animals have sensation
Therefore all giraffes have sensation

The point of such a syllogism is to explain the universal truth that giraffes have sensation, by referring to the fact that they are animals. Against this, Ibn Taymiyya pointed out that our knowledge is always grounded in encounters with particular things, and that universal judgements are generalizations from such encounters. Isn't it as good or even better, then, to use judgements about particulars in our reasoning, as the jurist does? Besides which, as even the philosophers agreed, the best thing of all to know about is God, and He is not universal, but particular.

Some of the points Ibn Taymiyya made in his *Refutation* had already been made by authors with a friendlier attitude to philosophy and logic, like Suhrawardī and Fakhr al-Dīn al-Rāzī. They wanted to revise but not abandon logic as they found it in the Aristotelian *Organon* and, above all, in Avicenna. Avicenna himself had radically rethought Aristotelian logic, not least with new ideas about modality (that is, necessity, contingency, and impossibility). After him, logicians continued to notice and fill gaps in the system. They noticed, for instance, that many perfectly good inferences cannot be put into the form of an Aristotelian syllogism. One much-discussed example was the 'relational' syllogism, for example:

> The Eiffel Tower is bigger than the elephant
> The elephant is bigger than the mouse
> Therefore the Eiffel Tower is bigger than the mouse

Right down through the late Ottoman empire we find authors attempting to extend the resources of Aristotelian–Avicennan logic to deal with inferences like this (for another example of developments in logic, see Box 7).

Box 7 The liar paradox

The famous liar paradox, first discussed in antiquity, turns on self-referential assertions like 'this statement is false'. If that statement is false, then it is true; but if it is true, then it is false. In the Islamic world, this paradox already received attention from early *mutakallimūn*. They posed the question whether someone who had never before told a lie, and then states, 'I am a liar', counts as a liar or not. Later on, in the post-Avicennan period, many philosopher-theologians offered analyses of the paradox. Some proposed that 'this statement is false' is actually neither true nor false. For instance al-Ṭūsī argued that the truth or falsehood of a sentence depends on whether what it says about *something else* (not itself) is accurate. Unfortunately this solution would make it

Box 7 Continued

impossible to make any true or false self-referential statements; yet it surely looks true to say, 'this statement is in English', and false to say, 'this statement is in German'. The liar paradox was further debated by the philosophers at Shīrāz. One of them (the elder Dashtakī) suggested distinguishing between first- and second-order truth. Normally, he pointed out, one sentence can be about another sentence without causing any problems. If I say, 'what Mary says is false', then I have made a second-order statement, that is, a statement about a statement. In that case, what I say will be true just when what Mary says is false; this causes no difficulty. The problem is that in the liar case, the sentence is about its own truth or falsehood, so that we do have the possibility of inconsistency between the first- and second-order levels.

In the long run, and despite the complaints of critics like Ibn Taymiyya, logic became a standard part of the education of religious scholars across the Islamic world. Just like beginning philosophy students in late antique Alexandria, students at *madrasas* in early modern India, Persia, or Egypt would encounter logical textbooks early in their studies—not a work by Aristotle or the *Introduction* of Porphyry, but a post-Avicennan logical treatise like al-Kātibī's *Risāla*.

The supremacy of reason

The most confident, even aggressive stance taken in favour of philosophy in the Islamic world is to be found in al-Fārābī and in authors influenced by him, especially Averroes. Al-Fārābī begins from the idea that we want to achieve *certainty*. In a short treatise on this subject, he acknowledged that there may be different degrees of certainty. I might, for instance, count myself as having 'certainty' that Avicenna's real name was Ibn Sīnā because I read it in a book from a reputable publisher. But the highest degree of certainty, which al-Fārābī calls 'absolute certainty', cannot be acquired through this sort of second-hand information gathering. Nor can absolute certainty even be concerned with such things as Avicenna's real name. Absolute certainty is a feature of knowledge in the strict sense, or 'science (*'ilm*)', which means being certain about universal and necessary truths.

How then to achieve certainty about such truths? Al-Fārābī's answer was *burhān*, or 'demonstration'. *Burhān* was also the name given to the Arabic version of the *Posterior Analytics*, in which Aristotle set down the requirement that scientific truths should be necessary and universal. In line with Aristotle's theory, al-Fārābī thought that demonstrations are syllogistic arguments that yield the appropriate, scientific sort of truths as conclusions. The syllogistic argument explains why the conclusion is true, as we saw with the giraffe example. But of course a syllogism is only as strong as its premises. Suppose, going back to that example, that I wonder why it is that all animals have sensation? This appeared as a premise in our argument, but it may itself have a further explanation—for instance that all animals need nourishment, and require sensation to locate that nourishment.

There is a threat of regress here. It would be troubling if every explanatory demonstration stood in need of further demonstrations to explain why its premises are true. To avoid this, Aristotle and his followers invoked first principles, truths which stand in no further need of explanation. These principles, which might be basic rules of reasoning like 'the whole is greater than the part' or general facts about the world gleaned from sensation, provide the foundations upon which Aristotelian science rests. Another member of the Baghdad school, Ibn 'Adī, used this idea to explain logic's role as an 'instrument for philosophy'. The inference rules of Aristotle's syllogistic tell us how to combine first principles into valid arguments. These arguments securely establish further truths, which can then be further combined using the logical rules, to derive even more truths.

When it comes to human beliefs, first principles and demonstratively proven conclusions are the gold standard. But al-Fārābī was prepared to hand out silver and bronze medals too. After all, as he himself admitted when he allowed for different degrees of certainty, not all true human beliefs reach the standard realized in demonstrative science. We routinely rely on testimony and on widely held beliefs, and accept arguments that we find merely persuasive rather than probative. Al-Fārābī looked again to the Aristotelian *Organon* to understand these sorts of beliefs. When we argue on the basis of assumptions or commonly held opinions, we are engaging in 'dialectic', which is studied in the *Topics*. Merely persuasive arguments, meanwhile, are classified as 'rhetorical'—no prizes will be awarded for guessing which Aristotelian work deals with these.

With these distinctions in hand, al-Fārābī was ready to make a bold proposal about the relation between philosophy, theology, and religion. A prophet who brings revelation to his people would not get very far if he presented them with demonstrative syllogisms. So instead, he speaks to them with powerfully convincing images and symbols. In other words, the language of revelation is characteristically rhetorical. As for dialectical arguments, which simply presuppose premises rather than tracing them back to rock solid first principles, they are in al-Fārābī's eyes typical of *kalām*. This does not, of course, mean that the *mutakallimūn* were always arguing for false conclusions. For instance al-Fārābī would agree with the Muʿtazilites that God exists, is one, is incorporeal, and is the first cause of all things. It's just that the *kalām* arguments for these conclusions were not demonstrative.

These ideas were taken forward in Andalusia by Averroes, in his *Faṣl al-maqāl*, usually translated *Decisive Treatise*. Here Averroes wrote from the point of view of a jurist. (He came from a family of Mālikī legal scholars and was himself chief judge in Córdoba.) Islamic legal judgements often addressed the question of whether a given activity is required, encouraged, licit, discouraged, or forbidden. In the *Decisive Treatise* Averroes applied this sort of question to philosophy itself. On the basis of Qurʾānic injunctions like 'take heed, you who have eyes' (59:2), Averroes inferred that the revelation instructs believers to seek knowledge. And what is philosophy, if not the search for knowledge? Thus philosophy is not just licit or encouraged, but actually *required* for Muslims, albeit only for the few who have the talent and opportunity to travel the daunting path towards scientific understanding. Other Muslims must content themselves with true beliefs induced by persuasion. Averroes agreed with al-Fārābī that this sort of belief is appropriate for the normal religious believer, and that *kalām* operates with dialectical arguments. Such argumentation could be dangerous. Averroes complained that the dialectical procedures of the theologians did not converge on agreement, leading to strife, and even violence, within the community.

Averroes was *not* saying that there are two different, even inconsistent, sets of beliefs, one for the philosophers and another for everyday believers. Rather, both groups have the same core of true beliefs. It's just that the philosophers have certain knowledge attained through demonstration, whereas the rhetorical class of believers are persuaded of things they can't prove, and grasp the truths symbolically. The normal believer may understand God to be powerful by picturing Him on a throne, whereas the philosopher can prove that He is the First Cause of the physical universe. This is another reason why it was unwise for the *mutakallimūn* to debate the meaning of the revelation publicly. It could confuse the rhetorical class to hear the theologians arguing for God's incorporeality. Exegesis of the Qurʾān should instead be left to the philosophers. They are the only readers who can be sure to interpret the revelation's true meaning, since they can check their interpretations of scripture against what they already know to be true on independent grounds. They should, however, go about this quietly, being careful not to shake the convictions of other Muslims (for a related dispute within Judaism, see Box 8).

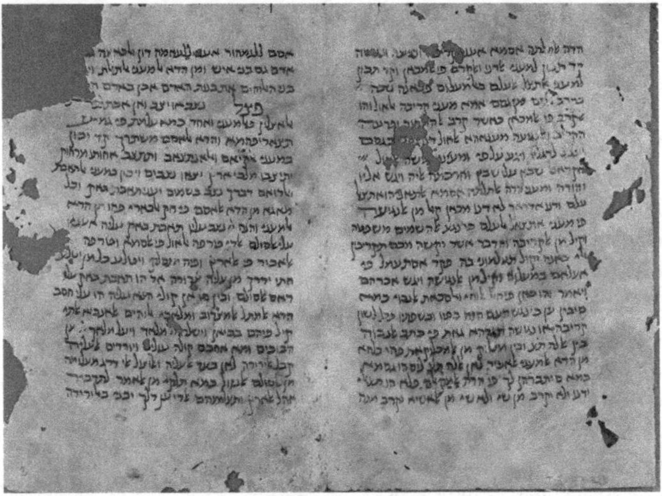

6. A manuscript from the Cairo Genizah, which preserves Maimonides' own handwriting.

Box 8 The principles of the Jewish Law

Like al-Fārābī, Maimonides (see Figure 6) believed that knowledge should have a foundational structure. He applied this to the Jewish Law itself, identifying a group of thirteen key principles upon which the rest of the Law was founded. Within this group of thirteen, three principles had particular significance: God exists, is one, and is incorporeal. Maimonides' attempt to give the Law this sort of scientific structure was challenged by a number of Jewish thinkers, both in Andalusia and in southern France. Maimonides' insistence that his co-religionists must deny the corporeality of God was already contentious. Kabbalistic authors indulged in bodily descriptions of God, and one of them remarked that many Jews, 'including Maimonides' betters', had taken such descriptions at face value. A different sort of critical response came from Ḥasdai Crescas.

Box 8 Continued

His remarkable assault on Aristotelian physics was staged in order to show the unreliability of Maimonides' argument for God's existence. Not, of course, because Crescas denied the existence of God, but because he feared that Maimonides was placing the Law on shaky foundations. He also questioned Maimonides' idea that we are *commanded* to believe the principles. Belief doesn't respond to commands, but to good reasons for believing. Later, the Spanish exile Isaac Abravanel (d. 1508) denied that the Law has any genuine principles at all. Rather it must be accepted through faith (*emunah*) in its entirety. Nonetheless, Abravanel thought that Maimonides' axiomatic approach could be justified on pedagogical grounds. One might start instructing a believer with so-called 'principles' before moving on to more specific aspects of the law.

The limits of reason

A prime example of the sort of public disputation that bothered Averroes was al-Ghazālī's *Incoherence of the Philosophers*. Its project is basically a negative one. Al-Ghazālī sought not to offer an alternative set of theories but to show that Avicenna's theories are unproven. This was not because al-Ghazālī rejected the desirability of certainty. To the contrary, the quest for certainty is a leitmotif of his intellectual autobiography, the *Deliverer from Error*. It describes an epistemological crisis he experienced as a young man, born out of considering the way that sense perception can be corrected by the mind. For example, shadows cast by the sun look to be standing still, but we know that they are moving very slowly throughout the day. How can we rule out that the judgements of the mind are likewise subject to some higher court of epistemological authority? Even the apparently indubitable truths of mathematics and logic could fall prey to this sort of sceptical worry.

Al-Ghazālī was freed from the impasse only thanks to 'a light cast into his heart' by God. The experience taught him that human reason cannot provide the highest form of insight and certainty. That is rather the province of the mystic, whose direct connection to the divine trumps even the most certain demonstrative argumentation. On the other hand, human reason is reliable in its proper sphere. The problem is not using reason, but thinking that reason can do too much, for instance by claiming to discern rules that would govern even the actions of God, as the Muʿtazilites and Avicenna had dared to do. Averroes would later charge al-Ghazālī with being 'an Ashʿarite with the Ashʿarites, a philosopher with the philosophers, and a sufi with the sufis'. While it's true that *kalām*, philosophy, and sufism all played a role in his thought, this does not necessarily mean that he was inconsistent. His willingness to take over ideas from Avicenna was tempered by his Ashʿarite commitment to the untrammelled freedom and transcendence of God, who is properly grasped only by the few who are granted mystical insight.

Another combination of philosophy and mysticism, though without the Ashʿarism, can be found in Suhrawardī. Explaining the methodology of his new 'Illuminationist' approach to philosophy, he said that it travels not one but two paths. One is the method of discursive enquiry and argumentation, characteristic of the 'Peripatetics'. The other was the higher road of mystical intuition, enjoyed not only by the sufis of Islam, but also by the sages of Greece, Persia, and India. They were all granted a direct vision of God, the Light of lights, and on this basis (supposedly) agreed on a range of doctrines taken over by Suhrawardī. As we'll see later, he also proposed a novel epistemology that could help to explain such mystical insights.

Al-Ghazālī and Suhrawardī set the tone for developments in the later Islamic world. Al-Fārābī and Averroes had claimed that certainty was the privilege of the philosopher alone, who achieves it through demonstrative arguments. Post-Avicennan theologians, including al-Ghazālī, agreed with them that certainty was an admirable goal. Whether that goal could be reached through nothing but human reasoning, though, was another matter. In the work of a theologian like Fakhr al-Dīn al-Rāzī, we see the full flower of the dialectical method characteristic of *kalām*. He did follow earlier *mutakallimūn* in also recognizing a type of knowledge as 'necessary', meaning that we cannot help endorsing it. But when it came to more contentious and difficult points, his characteristic method was to consider all the positions that had been (or could be) adopted on a given philosophical issue. In the end, all but one position would be shown to be incoherent or implausible. Scrupulous in his methodology, al-Rāzī would not always assert the certain truth of the victorious position, the one that has survived the process of elimination. Instead it might be designated as 'most adequate (*aqrab*)' among the options considered. When al-Rāzī concluded his arguments with the pious formula 'but God knows best', he meant it.

The later tradition of philosophical theology is a rebuke to the charge of methodological carelessness levelled at *kalām* by al-Fārābī and Averroes. Al-Rāzī was as much a rationalist as the philosophers, but more modest when it came to the question of what reason can establish beyond all doubt. This was entirely in keeping with the tenets of Ashʿarism, a tradition which would sometimes take refuge in the expression *bi-lā kayf*, or 'without saying how'. For instance some Ashʿarites would insist that God does have distinct attributes, but refuse to say how exactly we should understand these attributes and their relation to God's essence. Ashʿarite *kalām* did not necessarily go hand in hand with mysticism—al-Rāzī was no sufi. But in al-Ghazālī and certain other, later thinkers the epistemic modesty of the *mutakallimūn* did serve the ends of mysticism, as for that matter did limits on philosophical demonstration recognized by the philosophers themselves. Both *kalām* and Avicennan philosophy admitted that God remains, at least to some extent, beyond the understanding of natural human reasoning. So there was plenty of room to say that mystical insight must complement discursive rational argument.

The mystical tradition offered the prospect of going where reason could not. Sufi ascetic practices helped to direct the developing mystic's attention away from worldly things and towards the divine. Stories about the early sufi Rābiʿa al-ʿAdawiyya tell of her unconcern for the world around her and her yearning for God. She is said to have remarked, 'the love of God inhibits me from the love of His creatures'. The most famous sufi of all, the Persian poet Rūmī, famously used images of sex and drunkenness to convey the mystic's union with God. Ultimately, the sufi's goal was to achieve not some sort of discursive account of God, but rather an obliteration or annihilation (*fanāʾ*) of the self, in which the mystic dissolves in God's being, like 'a drop of vinegar in an ocean of honey'. Yet Rūmī did not abandon reason entirely. He remarked that 'the leg of the reasoners is wooden' and hence unsteady, but he also retained a significant role for 'intellect (*ʿaql*)', making it the capacity by which we grasp God.

The direct union with God achieved by the sufis promised to remedy the deficiencies of the philosophers' reason. But talk of union was dangerous, too. At their most provocative, the sufis could be taken to eliminate all distinction between God and what God has created—as when al-Ḥallāj notoriously remarked, 'I am the Truth'. Some, like Ibn Taymiyya, were quick to denounce this tendency among the more extreme sufis. But the sufis themselves were alive to the danger, and took pains to preserve God's transcendence despite recognizing His union with, or presence to, all other things. On this score, the greatest contribution was that made by Ibn ʿArabī, which was then systematized and fused with philosophical language by al-Qūnawī and other members of the 'Akbarian' school (an allusion to Ibn ʿArabī's epithet *al-akbar*, 'the greatest'). Ibn ʿArabī made much of the divine names found in the Qurʾān, seeing them as the means by which God made Himself manifest to His creation. Had the names not been revealed to us, we could not speak of God at all. But the divine names are more than mere labels. They are the very relationships that God bears to created things, and ultimately identical with those things. The created universe is distinct from God, and characterized by multiplicity rather than God's total simplicity, in just the way that God's various names are distinct from Him and form a multiplicity. God in Himself, though, remains beyond all that He has made.

There is a strong parallel between these ideas and the Jewish mystical tradition of Kabbalah, which is most likely no coincidence. Kabbalah emerged from the same cultural context that produced Ibn 'Arabī, and may have been influenced to some extent by Islamic mysticism. The *sefirot* of Kabbalistic theory play a role akin to the divine names in Ibn 'Arabī's thought, symbolically evoking the emanation of God's influence into the created world. Again, God Himself remains beyond our grasp. He is, as the Kabbalists of southern France put it, the *ein sof* or 'infinite'. This sefirotic theory looks to be a kind of theoretical account of God's relationship to the universe. But this was only one aspect of medieval Kabbalah. Again like sufism, Jewish mysticism also had a practical dimension, with ritualistic and meditative practices designed to provoke the experience of union with the divine.

The mystics themselves noted that their enterprise transcended religious boundaries. We've already seen Suhrawardī claiming common cause with sages from multiple traditions, both within and outside Islam. Two thinkers of Islamic India, the Mughal prince Dārā Shikūh and Shah Walī Allāh, had a similarly ecumenical outlook. Particularly striking is Dārā Shikūh's treatise *The Confluence of the Two Oceans*. The title refers to the agreement between the traditions of Islam and classical India, as represented especially by the *Upanishads* (which Dārā translated himself). The *Confluence* lists correspondences between Sanskrit philosophical terminology and the technical terms of philosophical sufism, and argues for the agreement of the two traditions on points such as the nature of the soul and bodily resurrection. Dārā thus took very seriously an injunction he found in one Hindu sage, to the effect that the truth does not belong solely to any one religion.

Of course none of this deterred philosophical sufis from a profound engagement with Islam and its key texts. Shah Walī Allāh's ecumenicism was tempered by his insistence that Islam is the most perfect manifestation of the truth shared by all religions. And if we consider another great philosopher of recent centuries who drew on sufism, Mullā Ṣadrā, we find a thinker whose thought and writing is steeped in the language of the Qur'ānic revelation. Like several other Muslim philosophers (notably Fakhr al-Dīn al-Rāzī), Ṣadrā wrote works of commentary on the Qur'ān and saw no tension between this activity and the pursuit of philosophy. Ṣadrā wove concepts from the philosophical and sufi traditions into his exegesis. He echoed Ibn 'Arabī's idea that the divine names are manifestations of God and even applied this to the Qur'ān itself. The revelation is God's word, and thus contains within it all of creation (*al-sūrat al-fātiḥa*, the first or 'opening' chapter, in turn contains within it all that is expressed in the rest of the Qur'ān). Ṣadrā's innovative metaphysics was ultimately an attempt to explain God's creation as an unfolding or manifestation of what, in God, is perfectly unified.

Chapter 3
God and being

'There is no God but God, and Muḥammad is His Prophet'. This is one version of the Muslim profession of faith, or *shahāda*, which one utters when converting to Islam. The first part of the *shahāda*, beautifully alliterative in Arabic (*lā ilāha illā Allāh*), sets out the fundamental Islamic belief in God's oneness, or *tawḥīd*. Muslims, like Jews and Christians, recognize no other divinities but the all-powerful Creator of the universe. This might seem to make pagan philosophy a poor match for the Abrahamic religions. After all, we associate ancient paganism with a pantheon of multiple gods. But the philosophical treatises that came into Arabic-speaking culture thanks to the 'Abbāsid translation movement typically recognized a single first cause of all things, even if those treatises also spoke of other, inferior supernatural principles too. The *falāsifa* accordingly had no hesitation in using Hellenic sources to argue for, and explicate, the doctrine of *tawḥīd*, taking them as a jumping-off point for their own original ideas.

God as the True One

The first *faylasūf* to exploit the potential of the Greek–Arabic sources for this purpose was al-Kindī. In his *On First Philosophy*, he portrayed God as 'the True One', free of all multiplicity. As an interpretation of *tawḥīd*, this goes well beyond the mere assertion of monotheism. But rigorous insistence on the simplicity of God has a significant advantage. Al-Kindī argued that all things in the created world must be characterized by both unity and multiplicity. Since God has only unity, He is radically different from created things, and this secures His transcendence. And as the source of unity for all other things, He is the first cause. There is an apparent disadvantage here too, though. It seems sensible to say that God has multiple features, if only because He is so variously described in revealed scripture. How can God be called both 'powerful' and 'knowing', for example, if He is wholly without multiplicity of any kind? After all, power and knowledge look to be two distinct features or 'attributes (*ṣifāt*)'.

Al-Kindī nonetheless argued in *On First Philosophy* that God's unity rules out *any* application of human language to Him. Here he drew on Aristotelian logical works, considering the various kinds of predication and showing how each of them would involve plurality. A genus like *animal*, for instance, may be a unity but also implies a multiplicity of species that fall under it (*human*, *giraffe*, *dog*…). Hence genera are inapplicable to the utter unity that is God. Apart from the logical works just mentioned, al-Kindī was here responding to the Platonic writings of Plotinus and Proclus translated in his circle (see Boxes 9 and 10). In them, he found a first principle that was totally without multiplicity, and a source for unity in other things. A further influence on al-Kindī was *kalām*. The Muʿtazilites too defended a rigorous interpretation of *tawḥīd*. They refused to accept the reality of attributes that were in any way distinct from God, fearing that this would yield a plurality of divine things (not only God but also His power, His knowledge, etc.). Not that these early theologians made so bold as to deny the validity of Qurʾānic language. Rather, they interpreted it in a way consistent with God's simplicity. An example would be the statement of Abū l-Hudhayl that God is powerful through a power that is not other than Him, knowledgeable through a knowledge that is not other than Him, and so on.

Box 9 Philosophical theology: the Greek legacy

For philosophers inspired by the Graeco-Arabic translations, two authors loomed above all others when it came to conceptions of God: Aristotle and Plotinus. Aristotle devoted parts of his *Physics* and *Metaphysics* to a first divine cause, a self-thinking intellect that gives rise to all motion in the universe. Plotinus by contrast postulated a whole hierarchy of principles beyond the physical cosmos, at the top of which was an utterly simple first cause, 'the One' or 'the Good'. In one of several disagreements with Aristotle, Plotinus made the One not an intellect but superior to a second, intellective principle—on the basis that even a self-thinking intellect would be multiple, since it would be both that which is thinking and that which is being thought. While some *falāsifa*, such as al-Fārābī and Avicenna, adhered to the Aristotelian line and made God a thinking being, al-Kindī preferred Plotinus' view and insisted that God is beyond intellection. A further challenge for the project of combining Aristotle and Plotinus with Abrahamic religion is that neither of them really envisioned their first cause as a *creator*. Aristotle presented his god as a cause of motion, not existence, and Plotinus' One/Good was (naturally enough) above all a source of unity and goodness. Of course, nothing can exist without being one, so al-Kindī could follow the Plotinian understanding of the first cause as a source of unity and still think of God as a creator. But new conceptual tools were needed to clarify what it would mean for God to be a cause of existence—tools which would be provided by Avicenna.

This sort of position can be found early on in the Jewish tradition as well, notably in the case of Saadia Gaon. Like al-Kindī and the Muʿtazilites, Saadia placed great emphasis on the perfect unity of God. He linked unity closely to immateriality. The ascription of multiplicity to God would imply that He is in some sense bodily.

Box 10 Neoplatonism and negative theology

At the end of one of his treatises, Plotinus gave some blunt advice for anyone seeking to grasp his transcendent first principle: 'take away everything'. Neoplatonic currents in the Arabic world accordingly pushed thinkers towards negative theology. We see this among the philosopher missionaries of the Ismāʿīlī branch of shiism, who took inspiration from the Arabic Plotinus. One of them, al-Sijistānī (d. *c.*971), went so far as to say that even negations must be negated—in other words we need to see not only that it is inadequate to call God 'good' or 'powerful', but also that it is inadequate to say that God is '*not* good' or '*not* powerful'. In the Jewish tradition, the most ostentatiously Neoplatonic thinker was Ibn Gabirol. Likewise drawing on Graeco-Arabic works derived from ancient Platonism, he presented God as a simple One, transcendent above intellect. The complexity of all things other than God can be captured by saying that they have a 'material' aspect. Even incorporeal things like intellect and soul are made up of a 'spiritual' kind of matter, which receives determination by form. This doctrine of 'universal hylomorphism' (meaning that all things apart from God have both matter and form) was frequently attacked in Christendom, where Ibn Gabirol's *Fountain of Life* was well known in Latin translation.

For the same reason, God lies beyond the reach of human cognition. For all human knowledge derives from sensation, which grasps only bodies. We can however come to an indirect understanding of God, by perceiving that the universe must have a Creator. From here we may make a further inference: God is not only one, but also living, knowledgeable, and powerful. These characteristics are inextricably connected with the ability to create. However, we do not actually have a multiplicity of attributes here. That, Saadia thought, was the mistake that led the Christians to their dogma of the Trinity (with life, knowledge, and power being represented by the three Persons). To avoid this error, we should say that in God's case these features are perfectly united. It is only human language that leads us to distinguish them from one another as distinct attributes.

The idea that God is understood only indirectly, and on the basis of what He has created, reappeared later in the Jewish tradition. Maimonides' *Guide of the Perplexed* sought to resolve the apparent clash between the philosophical understanding of God and the language applied to God in the Bible. The philosophical account makes God simple, immaterial, and transcendent—indeed, beyond the reach of human language—whereas the Bible routinely describes Him with words that can apply to created things. Maimonides proposed a multi-pronged strategy for interpreting such descriptions. First, superficially positive attributes can be understood as concealed negations. When we call God 'good' we might mean that He is not evil; to call Him 'knowing' is simply to say that He is not ignorant. So understood, these 'positive' attributes fit into Maimonides' project of negative theology, since they do not actually apply human language to the divine. Other attributes, meanwhile, can retain their positive meaning so long as they are referred to the created world rather than God. If we say that 'God is providential', we are despite appearances speaking about the universe, which is here indirectly described as well ordered. Finally, there is biblical language that must be read allegorically or symbolically. If God is called a 'lion', this should be taken as a metaphorical way of saying that He is powerful. Of course, we can't take 'God is powerful' at face value either. Instead, we should now apply one of the first two strategies to the statement yielded by the symbolic interpretation. Thus the upshot of saying 'God is a lion' might be something like 'God is not weak'.

God as the necessary existent

The single most influential philosophical argument to emerge in the Islamic world was Avicenna's proof of God's existence. Known as the 'demonstration of the truthful (*burhān al-ṣiddīqīn*)', it was gratefully received by philosophers of various faiths, and even endorsed by theologians who rejected other aspects of Avicenna's philosophical theology. Thanks to his proof, it became standard in the post-Avicennan Islamic tradition to call God the 'necessary of existence (*wājib al-wujūd*)'. This was the point of Avicenna's argument: to show that there must be at least one necessary existent.

Let's begin our look at the proof by asking what it would mean for something to exist *without* being necessary. Obviously, such a thing is not in itself impossible, since that would mean that it couldn't exist at all. Rather, it will be contingent. This means that the thing's nature, or as Avicenna would say, its 'essence (*māhiyya*)', does not settle the question of its existence. Avicenna gave the example of a triangle. Some things are required by the essence of a triangle, for instance having three sides, or having internal angles that sum up to 180 degrees. But existence is not one of them. We cannot tell, just by thinking about what it means to be a triangle, whether a triangle exists or not. Such contingent things require an external *cause* to make them exist. For Avicenna the cause 'tips the scales' by settling the question of whether it will exist or not. A genuine cause will in fact *necessitate* existence for the effect. To sum up: for Avicenna contingent things in themselves neither exist nor fail to exist, but become 'necessary through another' when they are determined to exist thanks to an external cause.

By contrast, a thing that is 'necessary of existence through itself' would be something that must exist by its very essence, without requiring any external cause. This brings us to the question answered by Avicenna's famous proof: is there in fact such a thing? Is anything necessary of existence in itself? Or are all existing things merely contingent, having received their existence from an outside cause? Avicenna wanted to show that this cannot be the case, and argued as follows (I've simplified slightly). Instead of taking just one contingent item, instead consider the entire aggregate of things that are contingent in themselves. This will be the set of all contingent things that exist now, ever have existed, or ever will exist (see also Box 11). Upon cursory reflection, we see that this aggregate is itself contingent. It *can* exist, and indeed it *does* exist—to be convinced of this you need only look around at

Box 11 Mental existence

Avicenna distinguished between two kinds of existence: mental and concrete. Usually when we talk about existence, we are thinking about concrete existence, which is just the reality of things out in the world. But things can also exist in the mind, in which case they have merely mental existence. Typically, a certain essence will have both kinds of existence. Giraffes, for instance, exist both concretely and in the mind. But some essences lack concrete existence, and exist only mentally—centaurs, for example. This apparently rather basic point had wide-ranging consequences in post-Avicennan philosophy. In the dialectical to-and-fro of philosophical *kalām*, it tended to stack the deck in favour of sceptical positions. With Avicenna's distinction in hand, authors like Fakhr al-Dīn al-Rāzī could demand proof that a given entity (time, for example) really exists concretely, as opposed to merely mentally. Later, in the Mughal era of Islamic rule in India, a series of commentaries on the *Ladder of the Sciences* by Muḥibballāh al-Bihārī (d. 1707) asked whether God as He exists in the mind might have different properties from those that God actually possesses in reality. He might concretely exist as simple, but exist in the mind with conceptual parts (if, as Avicenna argued, God is the Necessary Existent, then necessity and existence could be two parts). Generalizing the point, these Indian Muslim scholars posed the sort of general sceptical worry that was emerging in early modern Europe as well, to the effect that our mental concepts of things may misrepresent the way things really are.

all the existing contingent things. But the aggregate *needn't* have existed. After all, each member of the aggregate could have failed to exist, so surely the aggregate as a whole could likewise have been non-existent. This means that the aggregate requires an external cause in order to make it exist. And if that cause is *external* to the set of things that are contingent in themselves, then the cause is not itself contingent; it must therefore be necessary in itself.

Does Avicenna's proof work? It could be attacked at various points. One might challenge the assumption that the whole aggregate of contingent items needs a further cause. After all, if each individual contingent item within the aggregate has a cause, then why do we also need a cause for the aggregate itself? To make the objection more concrete, consider an infinite series of mothers and daughters that has led up to your mother. (This example is faithful to Avicenna: he believed that the universe is eternal and that the species of things have always been the same, so that the human race has also existed eternally.) Each woman has a mother, and we do not demand some external mother for the whole infinite series of women. It's a moot point whether similar reasoning would apply to the whole aggregate of existing things. But the popularity of Avicenna's proof shows that many philosophers shared his basic intuition, namely that the universe of contingent things could indeed have failed to exist, and that its existence thus stands in need of an explanation.

Another difficulty for Avicenna was that if the proof does work, all it shows is that there is at least one existent that is necessary in itself. Without further elaboration, that looks like something an atheist could cheerfully admit. But Avicenna gave further arguments to show that the trait of necessity implies the other features we associate with God, for instance immateriality, eternity, power, goodness, and knowledge. This project actually occupies much more space in his various writings on philosophical theology than the initial proof. With typical ingenuity, Avicenna argued for instance that there can be only one necessary existent, since if there were two, then some external cause would be needed to distinguish the two from one another—but then they would be necessitated-by-another, rather than being necessary-in-themselves. The necessary existent must also be immaterial, lest it depend for its existence on its matter; it must be perfectly good, since goodness is implied by actual existence; and so on, through all the traditional divine attributes.

One can hardly help admiring the elegance of Avicenna's strategy, which is to extract the whole of traditional philosophical theology out of the core notion of necessity. But from the point of view of later detractors, like al-Ghazālī, Avicenna paid too high a price to achieve this theoretical simplicity. He made God not just necessarily existent in Himself—this much everyone was happy to accept—but necessary *in every way*. This meant that God could no longer be conceived along Ashʿarite lines, as a gratuitously willing agent who creates, rewards, and punishes as He pleases. In addition to such scruples about the scope of divine necessity, the basic distinction Avicenna made between essence and existence led to metaphysical difficulties. Are we really to believe that concretely existing things out in the world are somehow compounded of an essence and existence, as if these are two parts that have been combined into a whole? A major critic of this conception was Suhrawardī. He was later described as having endorsed the 'primacy of essence', in contrast to the 'primacy of existence' upheld by sufis and in due course by Mullā Ṣadrā. This label is misleading, since Suhrawardī in fact denied the external reality of both essence and existence. For him, the essence–existence distinction is a purely mental one, with no corresponding distinction in the things themselves.

Against the realist position, Suhrawardī pointed out the awkwardness of supposing that essences have some metaphysical status of their own that is neutral with respect to existence. In order for an essence to be real enough to be distinct from the existence it will receive, the essence would already have to exist! As for existence, to suppose that it is something real seems likewise to involve thinking that it exists. A regress looms: if my existence exists, then the existence of my existence presumably also exists, and so on, but this looks absurd. These arguments look fairly convincing. But Fakhr al-Dīn al-Rāzī, while not shy in criticizing Avicenna on other points, rose to the defence of a realist understanding of the Avicennan distinction. He blocked the regress of second- and third-order existences by reminding us why we postulate existence in the first place: because essences are merely contingent in themselves, and need some external cause to make them exist or not exist. Existence in itself is not a contingent essence, so it has no need to receive a further existence. Essences too must be real, since otherwise there would be no real distinctions between things out in the world.

A further debate erupted within the realist camp when it came to the application of the essence–existence distinction to God. The upshot of Avicenna's proof seemed to be that God, like created things, has an essence distinct from His existence. The difference would be that, while God's essence guarantees His existence, the essences of created things do not settle whether they exist or not. Unfortunately, this seems to undermine God's simplicity. No less than al-Kindī, Saadia, and so on, the Avicennans were committed to God's oneness, which might be thought incompatible with bifurcating Him into essence and existence. Al-Rāzī applied the distinction to God nonetheless, in order to retain a unified conception of existence. The same sort of existence belongs both to you, to me, and to God. The only difference is whether the existence comes from outside (as in your and my case), or from the thing itself (as in God's case).

Al-Rāzī's rival commentator al-Ṭūsī seized on suggestions in Avicenna that God, or His essence, is *identical* to His existence. On this basis, he suggested that there is only a sort of analogy (*tashkīk*) between divine and created existence. The existence that is identical with God is, obviously, not the existence that belongs to you and me. Instead, the existence we enjoy is merely a dim reflection of divine existence. The disagreement between al-Rāzī and al-Ṭūsī mirrors a debate that was going on in Latin Christendom at about the same time, provoked by reflection on the same materials in Avicenna. Thomas Aquinas defended an analogy theory of being very much like al-Ṭūsī's, while Duns Scotus, like al-Rāzī, asserted that being or existence is always the same, whether it belongs to God or created things. This is just one example of the impact of Avicenna's ideas across the spectrum of later medieval philosophy, both within and beyond the Islamic world.

God as the Light of lights

One of the more contentious questions in modern-day research on Avicenna is the extent to which he can be seen as a mystic. He certainly at least paid lip service to the sufi tradition, in a few places using such mystical terminology as 'taste (*dhawq*)' to describe our grasp of the divine. But Avicenna's real importance for the history of philosophical sufism lies in the adoption of his ideas by other thinkers. This began already with Ibn ʿArabī, who took over the Avicennan view that created things are made necessary through their cause. When it came to the question of existence, however, he and his follower al-Qūnawī distanced themselves from Avicenna to some extent. Seeking as always to emphasize God's transcendence, they portrayed the divine as a 'non-being' or 'nothingness' beyond created being. Even created things begin as 'non-existents', in that they reside in God's knowledge and power, waiting to be made manifest in the universe. Ibn ʿArabī uses the phrase 'breath of the merciful' to describe the things' emergence into being, an image that will be taken up by Mullā Ṣadrā.

At about the same time, another philosopher with mystical inclinations was rethinking Avicenna's metaphysics: Suhrawardī.

At first glance, his own metaphysics may seem to be little different, with talk of 'light' substituted for talk of 'existence'. God is now described as the 'Light of lights' which has no need of external illumination, and angels are luminous beings emanated forth from Him. Souls too are lights, immaterial and thus pure of the 'darkness' of bodies. While this does look very like the sort of emanative scheme put forward by Avicenna and before him by al-Fārābī, it would be a mistake to see light as a metaphor for existence. We've already seen Suhrawardī arguing against a realist understanding of existence: for him it is nothing but a mental judgment. Also, Suhrawardī insisted that his talk of light was not metaphorical. Souls, angels, and God are really lights, albeit not the sort of visible lights we see in the physical world. To call these things 'lights' is to say that they can become evident and known merely by being present, the way that visible light is seen whenever it is present to a healthy eye.

Centuries later, Mullā Ṣadrā and other Iranian thinkers who drew inspiration from him made enthusiastic use of Suhrawardī's light terminology and embraced the 'Illuminationist' label. This despite the fact that, on the key question of existence, Ṣadrā could not have disagreed more strongly with Suhrawardī. He was a realist concerning existence, and for him, talk of light and talk of existence were indeed interchangeable. At the same time, he endorsed what had in the sufi tradition been called 'the unity of existence (*waḥdat al-wujūd*)'. This phrase intimates that all created reality is a manifestation of the one true reality, namely God. (This is not inconsistent with the philosophical sufis calling God 'non-being': that characterization simply distinguishes Him from the sort of being characteristic of dependent, created, manifested existence.) Things other than God are, as a sufi might put it, mere ripples upon the ocean of divine being. 'Unity of existence' went nicely with their idea that in mystical union, the self is obliterated. Such 'annihilation' is actually the dispelling of an illusory estrangement from God. As Rūmī put it, we are like shadows in love with the sun, which disappear in its light when their desire is fulfilled.

Such teachings threatened to eliminate all distinction between God and His creatures. To avoid outright monism, Ṣadrā reached for a conceptual tool first adumbrated by Avicenna, and then developed by al-Ṭūsī: analogical gradation (*tashkīk*). In Ṣadrā's hands, *tashkīk* provides a way to steer between, on the one hand, a monist identification of God with all other things, and on the other hand, a radical separation of God from His creatures. It's no wonder that Ṣadrā adopted Illuminationist language, because light provides him with the perfect metaphor. Like a brilliant light whose illumination dims only gradually, God is pure existence and His effects receive existence from Him in ever diminishing degrees. It is the difference in the *intensity* of existence that makes, for instance, a soul a different sort of being from a body. Furthermore, as in the image of the radiating light, there are no sharp divisions between the degrees of existence—what we have here is a gradual fade to black, not a series of differently illuminated bands. Earlier sufis like al-Qūnawī had spoken of the 'specification (*ta'ayyun*)' of being that occurs when God's infinite existence is contracted into the created things that are His manifestations. Ṣadrā can accept this too, but not if it is taken to imply that there are hard-and-fast distinctions between those specified, created things. Rather, the distinctions we make between things are just that: distinctions *we* make. Here he agreed with Suhrawardī, in rejecting the concrete reality of essences. They are only mental constructs, conceptual boxes we use to divide the unity of reality into distinct, manageable items.

Surely, though, there is a difference between dogs and cats, between chalk and cheese? How can Ṣadrā think that such differences are mere illusions? Well, that would actually be putting the point too strongly. He was no full-blown monist, who denies all real diversity. Rather, he wanted to say that the diversity is gradual, due to the continuous reduction in the intensity of existence as it pours forth and away from God. This is true not only at any one time, but also over time. In a further radical move, Ṣadrā contends that all things are constantly changing, even in their very substance. He gives examples like boiling water, which is in the process of changing into steam, and an embryo, which is gradually becoming an infant. The point applies in less obvious cases too, for instance to you as you change moment by moment, from infant to child to adult to senior citizen. Characteristically, Ṣadrā seeks confirmation for his theory in the Qur'ān, which states: 'when you see the mountains you think they are stable, but they are fleeting just like the clouds' (27:88).

Ṣadrā's theory itself represented a decisive change. It was a shift away from the more or less Aristotelian metaphysics of Avicenna and most of his heirs, who still recognized that reality consists of self-subsisting substances demarcated from one another by their essences. Instead, Ṣadrā presented a dynamic picture of reality, according to which existence comes forth from God as a gradually differentiated unity, and also returns to Him through constant change. The intellectual ancestors of this theory were not Avicenna and Aristotle, but rather Neoplatonists like Plotinus, whose works received renewed attention in Safavid Persia in Ṣadrā's day. Despite these ancient resonances, though, Ṣadrean philosophy has remained relevant, especially in Iran, thanks to exegetes and defenders like Sabzawārī in the 19th century and Ṭabāṭabā'ī in the 20th century.

Chapter 4
Eternity

The issue most strongly associated with the history of philosophy in the Islamic world is the eternity of the universe. This is rather surprising. It's not exactly a pressing topic in philosophical discussions nowadays, after all. Besides, you might expect Muslim, Jewish, and Christian philosophers simply to assume that the universe is not eternal, but rather created. Yet the question of eternity deserves its prominence. It features in several key works from the Islamic world—notably al-Kindī's *On First Philosophy*, al-Ghazālī's *Incoherence of the Philosophers*, and Maimonides' *Guide for the Perplexed*—and relates to several other philosophical problems that are indeed pressing issues for us today, such as time, infinity, modality, and causation.

Infinity and eternity

What does it mean for something to be 'eternal'? A first approximation might be that something is eternal if it exists at all times. To call something 'eternal' in this sense is both an observation about past history and a prediction about the future: an eternal thing has already existed at all previous times, exists now, and will exist at all future times. But there is an ambiguity here. Suppose that time began only 100 years ago. In that case, something one hundred years old that will continue existing indefinitely into the future would be 'eternal' in the sense just suggested, since it would exist 'at all times'. But we might hesitate to call such a thing eternal, and instead insist that genuine eternity requires time to be infinite. With this presupposition in hand, something is eternal only if it has already existed for an infinity of time, exists now, and will continue to exist for an infinity of future time.

Both conceptions of eternity have their problems. To suppose that time began at some point in the past confronts us with the paradox of how time itself can begin. It seems irresistible to think that, beforehand, there would be earlier moments at which time did not yet exist. But this looks like a contradiction: how can there be moments without time? Unfortunately, assuming an infinite time yields an equally unappealing paradox. For we would need to suppose that an infinite past time has already elapsed in order that we may have reached the present moment. But how can an infinity of time elapse? Both puzzles were raised in antiquity. For Aristotle, the paradox to avoid was rather the first one of admitting that time began. Nor did Aristotle think it was possible that motion ever began. For any motion requires another motion to trigger it. In his technical language, the potentiality for any motion must be realized through some previous actual motion. Thus any putative first motion would need a prior motion that causes it.

These two points, concerning the infinity of past time and the impossibility of a first motion, are intimately connected. Aristotle thought that there can be no time without motion. According to his much-discussed definition, time is 'the number of motion in respect of priority and posteriority'. The impossibility of a first motion gives us a further reason to think that past time is infinite. If there has always been motion, then there has always been time measuring or numbering motion. Many representatives of the Abrahamic faiths would find Aristotle's eternalism incompatible with the idea of a Creator God. But it's worth noting that he used his claims about eternity to prove the existence of God.

An immaterial cause, he reasoned, would be needed to give rise to the infinite motion required for such an eternal universe. Of course, Aristotle's God was not a creator, at least not in the sense of making the universe exist after previously not existing. Rather, his God was a first cause of motion, in particular of heavenly motion, which then gives rise to the motions in our lower world below the heavens (see Box 12).

Box 12 The influence of the stars

Aristotle's idea that God directly causes celestial motion, and only indirectly affects our lower world, was taken on in a surprising way in the Islamic world. It became a rationale for the science of astrology, which could now be presented as the study of God's providential care for the universe. When we study the motions of the stars, we are examining the instruments through which God brings about His cosmic plan. This can already be found in al-Kindī and his colleague Abū Maʿshar, a major figure in the history of astrology. By associating the Aristotelian theory with astrology, they departed from the view of earlier exegetes like Alexander of Aphrodisias. Alexander too thought that God influences our world through heavenly motion, but only at the level of species. In other words, heavenly motion providentially ensures that humans, giraffes, and sunflowers are propagated from generation to generation, without being designed to cause particular events involving this or that individual. Yet precisely these sorts of events were at stake in astrological prediction. Philosophical debate would continue in subsequent centuries, for instance among Jews in Andalusia. Here Abraham ibn Ezra was a strong proponent of astrology, who even explained the misfortunes of the Jewish people with reference to the malign influence of Saturn. Similarly Abraham ibn Daud wrote of the stars as the 'servants of God's decree'. Not long after, though, Maimonides was highly critical of astrology. In a letter on the topic written to a Jewish community in Provence, Maimonides

Box 12 Continued

went so far as to blame the destruction of the Jewish temple on the fact that Jews were distracted by astrological pursuits. He preferred Alexander's position that heavenly motion gives rise to the continuity of species, rather than individual events.

In late antiquity, the Christian John Philoponus argued vigorously against Aristotle's eternalism. In this context he invoked our second paradox: that an infinite past time cannot finish elapsing in order to reach the present. His anti-eternity works were known in the Arabic world, and were used by al-Kindī and Saadia Gaon. Taking up Philoponus' polemic, they argued that the physical universe cannot be eternal if, as Aristotle believed, it is finite in size. For Aristotle, the cosmos has an outermost limiting body which is spherical in form. In this outermost sphere are embedded the so-called 'fixed stars', while the planets are seated upon lower spheres arranged concentrically around the earth. Al-Kindī and Saadia broadly accepted this Aristotelian description of the cosmos, but turned it against Aristotle himself. Nothing finite can have properties that are infinite, they argued, so a universe of limited size cannot have a power to exist for an unlimited time.

Ironically, it was precisely on this basis that Aristotle had proved the existence of God. Since the celestial motion is infinite in time, it cannot be explained with reference to the finite cosmos itself, but requires an immaterial cause. The upshot is that there were two, mutually incompatible paths from the finite size of the universe to the existence of God. One could, with Aristotle, say that this finite cosmos exists eternally, and requires God to make it move for an infinite time. Or with Philoponus, al-Kindī, and Saadia, one could say that a finite cosmos cannot be eternal, and therefore must be created—thus proving that there is a Creator. That God's existence can be proven either on the assumption that the universe is eternal, or on the assumption that is not, did not escape the notice of philosophers in the Islamic world. The point was made by Ibn Ṭufayl, who had his desert island protagonist Ḥayy ibn Yaqẓān use both methods of proof.

Another philosopher of Andalusia, Maimonides, provided a more involved discussion, contending in his *Guide for the Perplexed* that none of the arguments for or against the eternity of the universe is decisive. He assumed nonetheless that the universe is indeed eternal, for the sake of argument—the argument being one for God's existence, based closely on the reasoning used by Aristotle. This has occasioned some suspicion that Maimonides was in fact a convinced eternalist, but reluctant to say so. More likely, he saw the same point made by Ibn Ṭufayl, that God's existence can be proved on either assumption. Admittedly, Maimonides lavished more attention on the path from eternity to God than the one from non-eternity to God. But this was a reasonable strategy, since the latter path looks to be an easier one: if the universe is not eternal but created, then obviously it has a Creator.

Maimonides' nuanced approach did not please everyone. The *Guide*'s elaborate Aristotelian argument for God's existence was subjected to a searching criticism by the later Jewish thinker Ḥasdai Crescas. In the course of his critique, Crescas put forth a number of innovative ideas concerning physics and infinity. (Some of these ideas can also be found in the earlier Abū l-Barakāt al-Baghdādī, but it is unclear whether there is a connection between the two.) Aristotelians had always drawn a distinction between the sort of infinity involved in an unlimited physical magnitude and the one involved in eternal past time. A body cannot be infinitely big because it would be actually infinite. In other words, it would be an unlimited magnitude that is actually present in its entirety. But past time can be eternal, because it is only potentially infinite. This infinity is like the one involved in counting up through the numbers. When we count up, we need never come to an end, since we never reach a highest number. The same applies to the number of years that the universe has already existed.

Philoponus, al-Kindī, and Saadia thought that a past eternity would rather be an actual infinity, because an actually infinite number of moments, hours, or years must already have elapsed. Crescas took a startling and different tack, arguing that actual infinities are not absurd anyway. This is not to say that he actually believed the universe to be infinitely large. Rather, he was out to show that the Aristotelians have failed to rule out the possibility, along with several other hypotheses concerning the physical universe. Other examples included the possibility of an infinite void surrounding a finite cosmos, or of a succession of universes that come into and out of existence. Crescas thus rejected all proofs of God based on Aristotelian physics.

Time and eternity

Aristotle's influential definition of time as a measure or number of motion left the metaphysical status of time somewhat unclear. Time might be objectively existent, as a quantity that depends on moving bodies for its existence. Or it might be subjective, and need somebody to do some actual measuring of motion. (At one point Aristotle implied this, remarking that there would be no time without soul.) Though the subjectivist approach was not unknown in antiquity—Augustine is a famous example—most Aristotelians thought that time is objectively real. Its reality would however depend on the more fundamental reality of bodies, since there can be no motion without bodies. Likewise, it would only be through motion and change that we come to grasp time. Taking on a brief suggestion found in Aristotle himself, later Aristotelians gave celestial motion primacy in their account of time. Since this is the fastest motion, and is regular and unceasing, the temporal measure of this motion can serve as a standard for coordinating and measuring all other motions.

A rival view was set forth by Abū Bakr al-Rāzī, whose notorious theory of 'five eternals' makes time one of the fundamental, uncaused principles of the universe along with God, soul, matter, and place. For al-Rāzī, temporal duration is not dependent on motion or bodies, but is a 'self-subsisting substance' in its own right. Nor do we need to experience motion to grasp that there is time. Rather, it is something to which we have immediate access. Contesting the rival Aristotelian theory, he invoked the intuition that time would continue passing even if there were no celestial sphere at all, and the fact that someone can be aware of the passage of time without being aware of motion. He also argued that time cannot be created by God, because that creation would have to occur at some time; thus time would need to be present before being brought into existence, which is absurd.

Al-Rāzī called his causally independent temporal duration 'absolute time' or 'eternity'. He contrasted it with the sort of time envisioned by Aristotle, which is at stake when we measure particular motions. Consider the way that, according to pre-Copernican cosmology, the sun revolves around the earth. One such revolution is measured by us as a single day. For al-Razī, this day is nothing but a demarcated segment of absolute time, which has always been and always will be elapsing, independent of the motion of the sun or anything else. It provides a background framework against which we can say that one motion or event is before, after, or simultaneous with another. So when al-Rāzī spoke of 'eternity', he did not have in mind timelessness, but infinite duration. The notion that something might exist beyond time had, however, already been explored in antiquity. For instance the late ancient Latin Christian author Boethius spoke of God as surveying past, present, and future from a vantage point beyond the passage of time—like someone seeing a whole landscape from a high mountain. Boethius was not known in the Arabic tradition, but he was inspired by earlier Platonist works that were indeed known. Both Plotinus and Proclus ascribed unchanging eternity to the universal Intellect envisioned in their metaphysical hierarchies, while time was assigned to the soul and the physical universe.

Drawing on this tradition, numerous philosophers of the Islamic world described God as being beyond time (for *kalām* views see Box 13). Al-Kindī gives us our earliest example, albeit only in a passing remark from his *On First Philosophy*: 'the First Cause is first in respect of time, since it is the cause of time'. This is rather

Box 13 *Kalām* views of time

An alternative to the Aristotelian view of time was offered by Islamic theologians. A commitment to atomism spanned the Muʿtazilite–Ashʿarite divide, with representatives of both schools affirming that there are smallest, indivisible parts of matter. These theologians also apparently thought of time as being composed of atoms, that is, smallest indivisible units. That allowed them to explain differences in speed, by saying that slower motions include a higher number of imperceptible pauses or 'rests' at indivisible times. All of this contradicted the Aristotelian physics accepted by most *falāsifa*, according to which matter, space, and time are continuous, that is, indefinitely divisible. The *kalām* authors also differed from the Aristotelians when it came to the definition of time. The Muʿtazilite thinker Abū ʿAlī al-Jubbāʾī (d. 915) proposed that time can be thought of as something 'stipulated' for the coordination of multiple events. For instance if I say, 'Zayd will come when the sun rises', then Zayd's arrival and the sunrise are being coordinated in virtue of a third thing, namely the moment or time at which both will occur. Though this is completely different from the Aristotelians' definition of time as a measure of motion, al-Jubbāʾī agreed with them that celestial motion has some claim to primacy in our understanding of time. According to al-Ashʿarī, al-Jubbāʾī stated that 'moments are the motions of the celestial sphere, because God stipulated them for things'. The example of Zayd and the sunrise would illustrate this: God has providentially assigned time to the regular and predictable celestial motions, and we can coordinate other events with those motions.

cryptic, but does express an obvious rationale for ascribing timelessness to God. If time is linked to or dependent on created things—as implied by the Aristotelian view that time is the measure of bodily motion—then time itself comes into existence along with the created universe. So time itself is created, and God must be above time, given that He created it. For Abū Bakr al-Rāzī this argument would fall at the first hurdle, since he did not make time dependent on bodies, motions, or changes, and in fact insisted that God must create anything at a time. For him, creation thus presupposes time rather than bringing time into existence.

Asserting God's timelessness could help to solve a standard argument against the eternity of the universe. Consider the situation prior to the moment of the universe's creation. It seems natural to imagine that there was an infinity of time prior to that moment, during which God was not yet creating. So, what *was* He doing? (This puzzle too was already discussed in antiquity, for instance by Augustine, who was tempted to answer: 'creating hell for people who ask such impertinent questions'.) A more rigorous way of putting the problem is this: how can God choose the moment for creating the world? All the moments in this infinity of time are equally suitable, so it looks like He would have to choose arbitrarily, or at random. But such arbitrary choice seems unfitting for a perfectly wise Creator. Al-Rāzī found this argument persuasive. One of his reasons for positing Soul as a eternal principle was that unlike God, Soul began in a state of ignorance, and so could unwisely and arbitrarily select a moment for the universe to begin. But by saying that God is timeless, one could avoid the argument entirely. There would be no infinity of moments prior to creation. Rather, moments and time in general would only exist once God has created them. This point was made by al-Ghazālī in his *Incoherence*, though as we'll see shortly, he believed that the argument can also be defeated without invoking God's timelessness.

Of course the idea raises problems too. The gravest difficulty is God's relationship to created things. How can a timeless God create one thing on Monday and another on Tuesday? How can He know that you are reading this book now, but were not reading it one hundred years ago? One answer was proposed by the Safavid era Iranian thinker Mīr Dāmād, one of the teachers of Mullā Ṣadrā. He took inspiration from Avicenna, who had distinguished between time (*zamān*), perpetuity (*dahr*), and eternity (*sarmad*). For Avicenna these words are appropriate to relations between different sorts of entity: 'time' in the proper sense applies only to relations between changing things, as one would expect given the Aristotelian definition of time. 'Eternity', by contrast, applies to relations between unchanging things. Between them we have 'perpetuity', which applies to the relations that unchanging things bear to changing things.

Expanding on this, Mīr Dāmād put forward his theory of 'perpetual creation (*ḥudūth dahrī*)'. God in Himself remains above time, since He is unchanging. Yet He can bear relations to created, changing things through a creative act which is not 'eternal' but 'perpetual'. Through this act, God brings forth things that were hidden within His eternal power. The creation comes 'after' God in the sense that it is causally posterior, but this has nothing to do with time. Temporal beforeness and afterness apply only to the created things themselves, here in our physical universe. So we can think of things as existing in three ways: as eternally hidden when they are 'with God', as contained within a perpetual creative act, and as fully manifest or 'existent' in time. All this helps to resolve our puzzle. We can now say that the relations God bears to created things actually belong to the perpetual act which is distinct from God Himself, who is timelessly eternal. Mīr Dāmād's account attracted criticism from a philosopher of Mughal India, Maḥmūd Jawnpūrī (d. 1652). He complained that Mīr Dāmād was basically imagining that the same thing is created twice, first perpetually in God's act, and then temporally in the world. If that were the case, then one and the same object would exist 'before' itself.

Necessity and eternity

Mīr Dāmād's theory of 'perpetual creation' finds a third way between two options that seem mutually exclusive. Intuitively, it seems that the universe must be either created or eternal, in the sense of having no beginning in time. This opposition was presupposed in the early arguments inspired by Philoponus and given by al-Kindī and Saadia. For both of them, asserting that the universe is eternal would immediately imply that God did not create it. Conversely, it would be incoherent to imagine a created but eternal universe. The same opposition was assumed in other early debates, for instance the one over the createdness of the Qur'ān, in which opponents of this thesis were routinely said to believe that the Qur'ān is 'eternal'. Mīr Dāmād was working much later, and no longer took it for granted that something created must have a beginning in time. What changed in the meantime?

The short answer, as so often, is Avicenna. His understanding of causation entailed that something could be caused to exist, despite existing for an infinite time. That may seem pretty obvious. We need only imagine a cause that is producing its effect forever. Al-Ghazālī, trying to illustrate this notion on Avicenna's behalf, gave the example of a finger that is eternally stirring water. In such a case we would presumably have no hesitation in identifying the finger as the cause and the water's motion as effect, without demanding that the motion must have begun at some point. But there was a significant philosophical obstacle to such a conception, namely that eternity had long been supposed to imply necessity. In fact, Aristotle argued for this point explicitly in his *On the Heavens*. The idea is a seductive one. Clearly, impossible things are things that never exist. Why not suppose that, conversely, necessary things are just those things that always exist?

In a sense, Avicenna would agree with this, but he would also say that it is put too simply. He distinguished between two kinds of necessity: that which is 'necessary in itself' and that which is 'necessary through another'. As we know, he conceived of God as the only thing that is necessary through itself. Of course this means that God does not come into existence. He is, rather, eternal and unchanging. From his key tenet that God is necessary in every respect, Avicenna inferred that God is not only necessarily existent in Himself, but necessarily causes all other things to exist. He has only one direct effect, which is an intellect associated with the outermost celestial sphere of the universe. This intellect, and further celestial intellects caused in a chain descending from God, are 'necessary through another'. In themselves, they would neither exist nor not exist, because they are contingent entities. But they are necessarily made to exist, whether directly or indirectly, by God.

As a result, whenever God exists—which is always—His effects will also exist. We might say that they are 'eternal through another': they acquire their necessity from a cause, and acquire their eternal existence along with that necessity. How then could Avicenna account for the fact that some things are not eternal? Since you and I, just as much as the celestial intellects and spheres, are the result of a causal chain proceeding necessarily from God, why don't we live forever? Avicenna's answer was that change, including generative and destructive change, is introduced by heavenly motions. Though those motions are eternal, they produce varying effects in the world below. For instance, the sun will at one point be further away from a given object, at another point nearer, so the object will be first colder and then warmer. The accumulation of such effects yields the things we see in the earthly realm, as complex substances are built up out of simpler material constituents. Sadly you and I are such complex earthly substances, and are thus subject to bodily destruction.

Avicenna's distinction between the necessary-in-itself and necessary-through-another was a conceptual breakthrough. It was gladly used by later thinkers, even those who were highly critical of him. Much of the criticism came from theologians of the Ashʿarite tradition, most prominently al-Ghazālī. This was only to be expected. Where Avicenna made God necessary in all respects, the Ashʿarites always sought to emphasize God's untrammelled freedom. Originally, this had formed a part of their critique of Muʿtazilism. The Ashʿarites denied that humans can use their natural powers of reason to discern any requirements or limits on God, for instance with respect to morality. If God chose to reward sinners and punish believers, that would be His prerogative; we know that He will do the reverse only because of His revealed promises to humankind.

Furthermore, *mutakallimūn* from both schools held that God constantly creates all things, sustaining them in existence and also creating their properties (or 'accidents') and actions. On the standard *kalām* view, an apple sitting quietly on a table needs God to keep creating it at every moment; God will also be creating its scent, colour, and so on. These creative acts are subject to God's will. For the Ashʿarites this meant that absolutely everything in the created world is subject to God's free choice. This is not just because God could in theory intervene to change things, for instance by miraculously turning the apple into a pear. Rather, God must actively choose at every moment to (re-)create things the way they have been. If we see stability and constancy in the world, it is simply because God has graciously and providentially chosen to create more or less the same things from moment to moment. The theologians connected this to the Qurʾānic statement 'you will find no variation in [God's] custom (*sunna*)' (17:77). Their position is often referred to as 'occasionalist', borrowing a term applied to similar theories put forward by modern European philosophers, such as Malebranche.

Avicenna's 'hands off' God, who causes necessarily and has only one direct effect, could hardly be less like the Ashʿarite God. The clash occupies centre stage in al-Ghazālī's trenchant refutation of

Avicenna, *The Incoherence of the Philosophers*. In al-Ghazālī's eyes, Avicenna's necessitarian beliefs amounted to apostasy from Islam, a crime that is in theory punishable by death. *The Incoherence* begins with a thorough discussion of the eternity debate, going over several of the arguments we have already considered in this chapter. Since his aim was to show that Avicenna's case remains unproven, al-Ghazālī concentrated on exposing the weaknesses in the 'philosophical' position rather than developing a positive theory of his own. Still, al-Ghazālī's Ash'arite sympathies are frequently evident, as he emphasizes God's unrestricted freedom and power. Consider, for example, his treatment of the argument that if God were to create the world with a first moment, He would have to make an arbitrary choice between equivalent moments. We've seen that al-Ghazālī had an easy solution available to him: there is no time prior to creation, and so no moments among which God would be choosing. Yet he chose a different response, insisting that making arbitrary choices is precisely the sort of thing God can do, given that He acts freely and not necessarily.

Behind this point lies a radically different conception of agency from the one adopted by Avicenna. Avicenna too thought that God possesses 'will', in the sense that He acts while Himself remaining uncaused. He does not even have a final end or goal that He seeks to achieve, since any final end would be a sort of cause for Him. Of course al-Ghazālī agreed that God's creative agency has no external cause. What he found missing in Avicenna's account, though, was the presence of alternative possibilities. If God cannot choose between multiple, genuinely open courses of action, then He is not free and in fact does not even count as a real 'agent'. He would be more like fire, automatically and necessarily giving rise to warmth. As an example of the sort of freedom he has in mind, al-Ghazālī asks us to imagine someone choosing between two identically appealing dates (fruits, not romantic assignations). It is possible to choose just one arbitrarily, and also rational to do so. In the same way, if God really did need to choose one from an infinity of equally appropriate moments for the creation of the world, there would be no obstacle to His doing so, nor would doing so besmirch His perfect wisdom. God likewise has the freedom to perform miracles, so that the supposedly necessary laws discovered in natural philosophy turn out not to be necessary after all (see Box 14).

Box 14 Miracles

A famous section of al-Ghazālī's *Incoherence* concerns the possibility of miracles. According to al-Ghazālī, this is something the philosophers deny, because of their understanding of causation. For them, a genuine cause necessarily gives rise to its effect. If contact with fire really causes cotton to burn, then the burning is a necessary consequence of that contact. Hence it would be impossible for God to intervene and miraculously save the cotton from burning—presumably not a casually chosen example, since the Qurʾān speaks of God miraculously saving Abraham when he was cast into a fire. Al-Ghazālī argued that our assumption of a necessary connection between cause and effect is due to a habitual expectation derived from past experience. We have previously seen fire touch and burn cotton, or things like cotton, and assume that burning will continue to occur in similar cases. There has been extensive debate about what al-Ghazālī meant to argue here. Some believe that he sought to uphold the occasionalist position of other Ashʿarites: all causation is exercised by God, so that even when there is no miracle it is God who is active. On this interpretation, when cotton does burn upon contact with a flame it is God who causes the burning, not the fire. A different interpretation holds that al-Ghazālī accepted the efficacy of what are sometimes called 'secondary causes', in this case the fire. On this reading, he wanted to say that fire does burn things but does not necessitate the burning, since that effect can always be thwarted if God intervenes. Since God has the power to trump any other cause,

Box 14 Continued

nothing apart from Him has the power to necessitate. In a sense, God would still be involved in every case of causation, but in non-miraculous cases only tacitly, in that He would need to refrain from intervening. It may well be that al-Ghazālī wanted to leave both options open, at least in this context: whether God does everything directly, or allows for secondary causation which He can override, the possibility of miracles is safely established.

Al-Ghazālī turns the tables on 'the philosophers' by contending that they, too, must admit that the universe has arbitrary features. This is one of several contexts in which he invokes the analogy between spatial and temporal extension. Just as God could have created the universe five minutes earlier, He could have made the universe five metres wider in diameter. Given the vast size of the universe this would make no practical difference. Thus the actual finite dimensions of the universe, no less than the specific finite duration of the universe, are a matter of arbitrary choice. In the same way, God could have chosen that the heavens rotate in the opposite direction, or selected different locations for the poles of that rotation.

This is one of the many arguments found wanting in Averroes' response to al-Ghazālī, *The Incoherence of the Incoherence.* Averroes accused al-Ghazālī of tackling difficult issues with merely dialectical arguments, which might confuse readers incapable of reaching demonstrative understanding. Furthermore, al-Ghazālī was equating the views of 'the philosophers' with the views of Avicenna, when in fact Avicenna himself had departed from correct Aristotelian doctrine on many points. On this more specific point concerning apparently arbitrary features of the universe, like its exact size, Averroes simply denied al-Ghazālī's initial premise. The heavens affect our earthly world through their motions, and even a slight change to the physical arrangement of the whole system would yield dramatically different results. By contrast, Averroes' contemporary Maimonides was impressed with the apparent contingency of the universe as we see it. He gave the example of the number of fixed stars. These are so numerous that one star more or less would presumably make no difference. One cannot definitively rule out that the stars must be exactly as many as they are, for some reason known only to God. But it seems unlikely. The universe is, then, probably the product of contingent choice. From this, we can infer (though not demonstrate) that the universe was most likely created with a first moment in time. For, as the Aristotelians themselves had always claimed, eternity is linked to necessity, and contingency to that which is not eternal.

In a later resumption of these disputes, the Ottoman sultan Meḥmed II invited two scholars to write competing assessments of al-Ghazālī's *Incoherence*. The winner, Khojazāda (d. 1488), broadly agreed with al-Ghazālī's stance. He too thought that Avicenna had strayed from acceptable teaching and the bounds of orthodoxy, and rejected the eternity of the universe. However, he pronounced himself unimpressed by al-Ghazālī's arguments. For example, he agreed with the Aristotelians that a past eternity would not constitute an actual infinity, but only a potential one. Thus Philoponus' claim that the present moment cannot have been reached without getting through an actual infinity has no force. Khojazāda proposed a clever improvement to the argument to make it more effective. The flaw in the argument is that past times are never all existent simultaneously, so the eternalist cannot be compelled to accept that past eternity yields an actual infinity. But what of the past times existing in God's knowledge? Since God knows the entire history of the world, all these times will be simultaneously present in His mind. And this *will* be an actual infinity. As Khojazāda himself admits, these past times will be only mentally existent, but that is enough to yield the needed absurdity.

Chapter 5
Knowledge

The second part of the *shahāda*, or profession of Muslim faith, states that Muḥammad is God's Prophet. Yet Islam does not make prophecy the unique prerogative of Muḥammad. He was rather the last in a long line of prophets that began with the first man Adam, and included figures of the Jewish Bible as well as Jesus. This helps to explain the history of toleration towards other faiths within the Islamic world: Jews, Christians, and other groups were monotheists in possession of a true revelation, and thus recognized as fellow 'peoples of the book'. This attitude could be extended even as far as the Hindu scriptures, as in the syncretic thought of Dārā Shikūh, who believed that the *Upanishads* were a genuine and fundamental revelatory text (he even detected an allusion to the *Upanishads* in the Qur'ān). Philosophers in the Islamic world thus saw prophecy as a repeated phenomenon, which they tried to explain in terms of a more general account of human knowledge. To understand the special access to truth granted to the prophet, one needs first to understand how humans normally gain access to truth. This in turn presupposes an understanding of the human soul, which is responsible for the act of knowing.

Knowledge and the soul

Most philosophers of the Islamic world followed Aristotle in granting souls to animals and even plants, seeing soul generally as the principle of life in an organism. Hence rocks and tables do not have souls, but sunflowers and giraffes do, since they are alive. Plants are capable of nourishing themselves, and engage in reproduction and growth. Animals additionally possess the power for sensation and locomotion. Humans have all these abilities too, but are distinguished by their rationality—which is why they, and not animals or plants, have a capacity for knowledge. In the *kalām* tradition, we find talk of an afterlife for animals, but the *falāsifa* normally reserved the prospect of life after death for humans. This immediately suggests a connection between a soul's rationality and its ability to survive the death of the body. That connection lies with the way that the soul's various faculties are realized. The powers characteristic of plants and animals—nutrition, reproduction, sensation, and motion—can only be exercised through bodily organs. Reasoning and intellection, by contrast, would not involve the use of the body.

This sort of position, which was broadly accepted (with many differences of opinion on the details) by most *falāsifa*, splits the difference between two approaches to the soul that were received from the antique tradition. On the one hand there was Aristotle. Though he did argue that intellection involves no bodily organ, he made soul in its entirety the 'form of the body'. This suggests an intimate relationship between soul and body, perhaps to the extent that the soul is destroyed upon the death of the body. On the other hand were the Platonists, for whom the soul is in itself a separate substance which already existed before its relation to the body. That relation was taken to be a fairly casual one. The lower powers such as nutrition and sensation would be projections of the soul's power into the body, rather than essential parts or faculties of soul on a par with rationality. The same sort of analysis was applied to the classical tripartition of soul found in Plato himself. In the *Republic* and *Timaeus*, Plato argued that the human soul has three aspects: reason, spirit, and desire, respectively responsible for the pursuit of knowledge, honour, and pleasure. This analysis of the soul was widely received in the Arabic tradition alongside the threefold analysis of the soul taken from Aristotle, into plant, animal, and human powers. It was standard to assimilate the two lists of powers, with the Aristotelian animal faculties equated with the Platonic 'spirit' and the vegetative faculties equated with the pleasure-seeking appetitive soul. Either way, reason alone was seen as having the prospect of continued post-mortem existence.

This view has its attractions, not least its reconciliation of Plato and Aristotle. But it also poses certain difficulties. It makes the rational soul, by which we gain knowledge, markedly distinct from the lower soul through which we actually interact with the physical world. Yet it seems obvious that our knowledge is based, at least partially, on just this sort of interaction. In particular, it seems that sense perception is an indispensable means of achieving knowledge (empiricists would say that it is the only means we have). This is not only common sense, but authoritative doctrine. At the end of the *Posterior Analytics*, Aristotle explains that the principles on which all our knowledge rests are gleaned through sensation. Yet Aristotle also provided grounds for suspecting the epistemic credentials of sensation. In the same work, he laid down criteria that must be met before we can say that we have knowledge in the strict sense—the sort of knowledge or understanding we achieve in science. (In fact, the corresponding Greek and Arabic terms *epistēmē* and *'ilm* can mean both 'knowledge' and 'science'.) One criterion is that scientific understanding must be universal. Knowledge of giraffes, say, concerns not this particular giraffe but giraffes in general. Clearly, though, sensation is directed towards particulars, not universals: I always see or hear this particular giraffe, not giraffes in general. This gave the *falāsifa* a further reason to wonder how sensation could contribute to our acquisition of knowledge.

Philosophers of the 'Kindian tradition' tended to follow Platonist sources and to emphasize the rational soul's separation from the body. They drew a correspondingly rigorous distinction between sensation and intellection. Al-Kindī himself stated that the human being is *only* his rational soul, which will survive after death. On the methodological front, he held that it is impossible to have knowledge of particular things, because of their constant change—knowledge, after all, should be secure and unchanging. Knowledge is rather an intellectual affair, and is directed solely towards 'universal intelligibles'. If sensation plays any role in bringing us to knowledge, it is only by prompting the intellect to engage in its distinctive activity—perhaps by recovering knowledge it has had since before birth, al-Kindī suggested, echoing Plato's idea that knowledge is not learned but 'recollected'.

The strong contrast between sensation and intellectual knowledge was later reaffirmed by Miskawayh. We have a treatise in which he argued against an unnamed opponent, who among other things claimed that our intellect is entirely dependent on sensation for its knowledge. Miskawayh denied this: if anything, it is sensation that depends upon intellect to correct it, as when we realize that we are experiencing a sensory illusion. And intellect has an activity 'proper to itself', through which it grasps principles of reasoning (like the principle of non-contradiction) and knows of itself that it is knowing. Proper understanding of universals too is a task for intellect, and not sensation. On the other hand, Miskawayh was more generous than al-Kindī in allowing some contribution from sensation. He recognized a process of 'abstraction' by which universal ideas are gleaned from the experience of particular things.

Miskawayh's appeal to the 'abstraction' of universal forms from sensible particulars had ample precedent. The same link between sensation and intellection was made in works by members of the 'Baghdad school' of Aristotelian philosophers. The last of these, a contemporary of Miskawayh, was Ibn al-Ṭayyib (d. 1043). While considering the abstractive process, he mentioned the worry earlier posed by al-Kindī: that sensible things change and are thus unfit to be objects of knowledge. For Ibn al-Ṭayyib, this was enough to confirm that real objects of knowledge are universal forms. However, things are not subject to constant and total flux but keep their character for some limited, but extended period of time. So we can derive an intelligible form like *human* from sensible encounters with humans, even if the intelligible form is unchanging whereas all particular humans are born and die.

An earlier representative of the Baghdad Aristotelian tradition, al-Fārābī, had raised a further worry about abstraction, a version of what is nowadays known as the 'problem of induction'. If I am trying to reach universal understanding of, say, giraffes, how can it be sufficient to inspect only one or two giraffes, or for that matter any number of giraffes? I might always encounter a giraffe who provides a counterexample to my previous generalizations. Thus, no matter how many vegetarian giraffes I meet, I cannot be totally sure that all giraffes are vegetarian. A similar example found in several philosophers of the formative period is that someone living in Africa might form the universal judgment that all humans are black. This judgment would fit with all their experience, but would still be wrong. How then can we justify the leap from particular experiences to the universal claims required in scientific understanding?

An answer was proposed by Avicenna, who spoke of *tajriba*, sometimes translated as 'methodic experience'. *Tajriba* is no mere one-off experience, nor a simple generalization from many such experiences. Avicenna criticized this sort of inductive reasoning, which could not license the sort of universal and necessary judgments demanded by Aristotelian science. What *tajriba* adds is the assumption of some underlying *cause* for the regularities we perceive through experience. Avicenna's favourite example was the scammony plant's tendency to purge bile. Through repeated tests, we know that scammony has this property—or at least, we know it about the kind of scammony we have been testing. On this basis we realize that this kind of scammony has a nature which explains its purging of bile. Yet this is only a step towards full scientific understanding, since it remains to determine why exactly scammony does have this effect.

Although Avicenna and the members of the Baghdad school wanted to secure a robust role for sensation in our acquisition of knowledge, they agreed with Miskawayh that there are special activities proper to the human intellect. One such activity mentioned by Miskawayh is what would nowadays be called 'second-order' knowledge: knowing that one knows something. In a treatise on the conditions that must be fulfilled in order for knowledge to count as 'certain', al-Fārābī said that 'absolutely certain' knowledge always involves knowing that one knows. This rules out cases of 'accidental' belief, like the case of someone who believes everyone is black merely because everyone they have met is black. Such a person could not know that his or her belief is true. Rather, one can take oneself to be absolutely certain only when one has perceived necessary and universal truths, and knows that one has done so.

The mind's ability to reflect upon itself, as when it knows that it knows, received unprecedented attention from Avicenna. He too made the point that knowledge is always accompanied by the possibility of second-order knowledge. But he also claimed that the human soul has a more fundamental kind of access to itself, namely self-awareness. The soul is, Avicenna claimed, permanently aware of itself, even when asleep! It is just that we do not remember having being aware once we wake up. Avicenna thought that this fundamental activity of self-awareness could help answer the question of what makes each individual the individual he or she is. After all, self-awareness is something that each person can have only of themselves. And if each of us constantly has self-awareness as a background condition of all their other mental activities, then this self-awareness can guarantee that each of us remains one and the same individual over time.

The same phenomenon was invoked by Avicenna in his famous 'flying man' thought experiment. We are asked to imagine that a mature, fully functioning human is created by God out of nothing. The human is in mid-air, his sight veiled and his limbs splayed so that he is not touching his own body. There is no sound or smell. In other words, this person is in a state of total sensory deprivation. Furthermore, he has just been created, so he has no memories of prior sensory experience. Avicenna asked what a person in this situation could know. A strict empiricist would say, 'nothing', thinking that all our knowledge comes directly or indirectly from sensation. But Avicenna thought that the flying man would be aware of his own existence. He took this as a pointer, not only to the ineliminable self-awareness that belongs to each human soul, but also to the soul's immaterial nature. After all, Avicenna reasoned, the flying man's soul is aware of itself, but not of his body. How could this be, if the soul and body were the same thing?

As has often been observed, the argument looks poor. Even if we grant that the flying man would be aware of his soul, the thought experiment does not prove that his soul is distinct from body. Perhaps, for instance, his soul is seated in his brain. In that case, in being self-aware the flying man is aware of his brain; yet he doesn't realize that the self of which he is aware is an aspect of his brain. (An analogous case: if you saw me on the street but did not know who I was, you would be aware of the author of this book without knowing that the person you are seeing is the author of this book.) Various expedients have been proposed to absolve Avicenna from having made this mistake. According to the one I favour, the argument is indeed a 'pointer' rather than a proper demonstration. It draws our attention to the fact that self-awareness requires no awareness of the body. This offers an improvement on the traditional Aristotelian understanding of the soul as the principle of bodily faculties. True, the soul is such a principle, but describing it in that way, as Aristotle did, only gives us insight into the soul's incidental relation to the body. Self-awareness, by contrast, gives us direct access to the soul itself.

Knowledge and intellect

So far, I have been using the word 'intellect' as if it were a label for the rational part of the soul. But in fact the *falāsifa* typically recognized further intellects outside the soul. Yet again, there was a potential conflict between Greek sources. Whereas Aristotle depicted God as the first of the numerous intellects who are responsible for the motions of the heavens, Plotinus and other late ancient Platonists envisioned a divine first principle beyond intellect. There's not much wiggle room here—either God engages in intellection or He doesn't—so rather than a clever reconciliation we see the *falāsifa* choosing between the two options. Al-Kindī argued in Plotinian fashion that God, being purely one, is free of the sort of multiplicity involved in an intellect's grasp of many universals. Others, including al-Fārābī, Avicenna, and Averroes, did think that God exercises intellection and accepted the existence of other intellects (sometimes equated with angels) that are related to the heavenly spheres.

All this is based on remarks made by Aristotle in his *Physics* and *Metaphysics*, not in his proper treatment of intellect, which is to be found in the third book of his *On the Soul*. There, Aristotle restricted his attention to the human power for intellection. Or did he? The answer depends on how we interpret the infamous fifth chapter of that book, which speaks of a 'productive' intellect that makes thought possible, just as light facilitates vision. It alone, adds Aristotle, is separate and immortal. The full history of how this chapter has been interpreted would not fit into a very brief (or even very long) introduction. But on any reading, the productive intellect is being contrasted to the sort of intellect discussed in the preceding pages. There, Aristotle talked about the human potentiality for knowledge—when we come to know, this potentiality is actualized, much as the power of sight is actualized when we see. Apparently the productive intellect is somehow involved in this process of actualization, by virtue of being itself always actual. Whether the productive intellect is a further aspect of the human mind, a superhuman intellect, or even God Himself, was one of the questions disputed in the tradition of commentary on the chapter.

The *falāsifa* converged on an interpretation that was as much a theory of the mind as an elucidation of Aristotle. It was expressed as a classification of different kinds, or states, of the intellect. Though the details differed from one author to another, it was standard to contrast our inborn ability for knowledge, or 'potential intellect', to 'actual intellect', the state we are in when we are actively knowing. Meanwhile Aristotle's 'productive intellect', now often called the 'agent intellect', was placed beyond the human soul, yet below God. Conveniently, the Aristotelian cosmological theory postulated intellects that are associated with the spheres of the heavens. Al-Fārābī was the first to take advantage of this by identifying the agent intellect with the intellect of the celestial sphere closest to the earth.

This theory, also adopted by Avicenna, assigned two parallel functions to the agent intellect. First, as suggested in Aristotle's obscure remarks, this superhuman intellect plays a role in human knowledge. When we achieve full-blown intellective knowledge, we are able to do so because of the presence of the agent intellect. It has an eternal grasp of all universal intelligibles, and when we too grasp such an intelligible we are drawing somehow on its assistance. The second role of the agent intellect is cosmological. It helps to actualize not only the human intellect, but also physical substances, like plants, animals, and humans. When a certain portion of matter has been 'prepared' in the appropriate way (for instance through the concoction of menstrual blood in the womb of a mother), a form is emanated from the agent intellect, as appropriate to the way the matter has been prepared. This explains why all members of a given species share the same form. All giraffes, for instance, have taken their forms from the same source, which is the form of giraffe in the agent intellect. Despite initial appearances, this is not a version of Plato's theory of Forms. In fact al-Fārābī, Avicenna, and Averroes all knew and accepted Aristotle's critique of that theory, and would have been horrified to have their theory of intellect equated with it. The key difference is that the intelligible forms in the agent intellect are the *thoughts* of that intellect—they are not paradigms existing separately from other substances.

Another misconception to avoid is that, with this theory, the *falāsifa* were abandoning the empiricist tendencies of Aristotle. True, the intellect can acquire some truths without sensory input, but these are quite minimal—basically, the primary rules of reasoning, such as 'the whole is greater than the part'. All other intellection is somehow based on sensation, which prepares the soul in a way analogous to the preparation of matter in the case of the generation of physical substances. That is, it makes the soul ready to receive form. Beyond this, though, we run into difficulties concerning the precise mechanics of intellection. There has been especially intense debate over Avicenna. The basic problem is that Avicenna seems to have had not one, but two, explanations for how forms arise in the human mind. One story is the same as that given by the Baghdad school: forms are 'abstracted' from experiences of particulars. The other is that the form is emanated into the human mind from the agent intellect when the mind knows, just as it emanates forms into matter when natural things are generated. Any interpretation should give weight to both the 'bottom up' abstraction story and the 'top down' assistance provided by the agent intellect, since Avicenna did speak of both. But scholars disagree about why exactly the agent intellect is needed in addition to sense experience and abstraction. (For Avicenna's equally controversial remarks on divine intellection, see Box 15.)

Speaking of contentious issues, we are now ready to consider one of the most notorious philosophical theses to emerge from the Islamic world: Averroes' position on the unity of the intellect.

Box 15 Knowledge of particulars

For all his influence, Avicenna was heavily criticized by later thinkers on certain points. In a much-maligned passage of his *Healing*, he argued that God has knowledge of all things, but only 'in a universal way'. Like his account of human intellection, this claim has been interpreted in various ways. I take Avicenna to be following the standard Aristotelian line on knowledge: in the strict sense, all knowledge (whether human or divine) grasps universal truths. The difficulty is whether God can apply His universal knowledge to particular things. If you know that all dogs are mortal, and can add that Lassie is a dog, then you can infer that Lassie is mortal. But you are in a position to add that second premise—Lassie is a dog—only through your engagement with changing, sensible things. Such premises are reached through a faculty like sensation rather than through pure intellection. How, as a pure intellect, could God possibly know such things? Yet if He does not know them, He will never be in a position to subsume particulars under universals; in other words He could not apply His universal understanding at all. Avicenna's solution is that God sits at the top of the causal chain which gives rise to the particulars. By knowing Himself as a cause, He is aware of the particular effects. Notice the deterministic implication: all particulars need to derive inevitably, albeit indirectly, from God. Otherwise He will apparently not be able to know about them.

Heavily criticized by Aquinas, and still greeted with disbelief by readers today, this position can be summarized as the claim that all humans share only one intellect. Each human who knows is simply partaking in the activity of that single intellect. Though this sounds scarcely credible, we should remember that it was perfectly standard to posit a single *agent* intellect for all humankind. In this context, Averroes' innovation was less shocking. He simply added that there is likewise only one *potential* or 'material' intellect for all humankind. And this makes a certain amount of sense. How, after all, can a single actual intellect be paired with an unlimited number of potentialities (one per human)? Furthermore, as we have been seeing, intellection is meant to be universal. And there is only one set of universals to be known. Anything grasped by just one human to the exclusion of all others would be particular to that human, not universal. The unity of the intellect guarantees that when the teacher conveys some universal truth to a student, the teacher and student are quite literally thinking the same thing. A final thing to note about Averroes' view is that he, no less than al-Fārābī and Avicenna, gave sensation a crucial role in his epistemology. It is the particular experiences we have, and the work that individual humans are doing to abstract universals, that guarantee the constant realization of our shared capacity for knowledge.

Prophetic knowledge

Let's now return to the issue of prophecy. How do the *falāsifa* use their general account of human knowledge to explain the special insight granted to Muḥammad and other prophets? Broadly speaking, their answer was that prophets are individuals who have attained more completely, and without effort, the same kind of understanding that other humans must acquire through laborious enquiry. We can observe this tendency already in al-Kindī. He touched on the nature of prophetic knowledge in a passage situated, rather unexpectedly, in the midst of an overview of Aristotle's works. The point of the passage is to contrast the human knowledge attained in philosophy to 'divine knowledge', which is of course superior. That superiority, however, is said to consist simply in its effortless acquisition by the prophet, and the concision and clarity of the prophet's expression.

For a more substantial account, we may turn to al-Fārābī (see Figure 7). Making more explicit what was, at best, only suggested in al-Kindī, al-Fārābī argued that a prophet is first of all a person whose intellect has been fully actualized. He has, through contact with the agent intellect, come to know all the intelligibles. In respect of intellectual knowledge, the prophet is nothing less, but also nothing more, than a perfect philosopher. The prophet does however possess an additional capacity that distinguishes him from a mere philosopher: a very powerful imaginative faculty. For al-Fārābī imagination is akin to sensation, in that it recalls and manipulates images taken from our experience of particulars. This makes it suitable for the special insights given to prophets, for instance their ability to foretell future events. Here al-Fārābī was anticipated to some extent by al-Kindī, who wrote a work on

7. Al-Fārābī as depicted on a banknote from Kazakhstan.

prophetic dreams which likewise makes the imagination responsible for this supposed phenomenon. Al-Fārābī further extended the idea to account for the prophet's role as lawgiver and bringer of a revealed book. It is the prophet's imagination that enables him to do this. A revelation suitable to be appreciated and followed by all the people cannot just lay out truths in the dry, technical form appropriate to philosophy. It must use powerful imagery and symbols. But since the prophet does have a perfect intellect, he has a full understanding of the truths that underlie the more user-friendly, rhetorically effective revelation he offers to his fellow humans.

Like al-Fārābī, Avicenna integrated an account of prophecy into an Aristotelian epistemology (on which see also Box 16). He spoke of the 'holy intellect (*'aql qudsī*)', which belongs to someone who possesses to a remarkably high degree a capacity also found in some non-prophets. This capacity is known as 'intuition (*ḥads*)'. An intuitive person is able to solve problems in science by finding the 'middle term' that will connect two other terms in a syllogism in an explanatory way. For instance if one is wondering why frogs lay eggs, one may intuitively hit upon the explanation that frogs are amphibians—and this insight may come, as it were, 'out of the blue'. Quite likely Avicenna himself had this experience and devised his theory of intuition to account for it. The prophet is simply a more extreme case. He has intuition to a maximum degree and receives the intelligibles from the agent intellect either 'all at once or nearly so', as Avicenna puts it.

For both al-Fārābī and Avicenna, the prophet's reception of his insights, in both his intellect and his imagination, is 'automatic'. By this I mean that they occur for the prophet just by virtue of his being apt to receive them, much as matter, when suitably prepared, will automatically receive form from the Agent Intellect. This is a remarkably naturalistic theory of prophecy, and also a very general one, suitable for use in other religious traditions. It was duly taken up by Jewish thinkers of Andalusia, notably Ibn Daud and

Box 16 Inner senses

The *falāsifa* frequently contrasted sensation and intellection, the former suited to perception of changing particulars, the latter used for grasping eternal and universal truths. But this leaves out a good deal of our mental life. When we remember what we had for breakfast, wonder what to have for dinner, or have unsettled dreams after having chosen spicy food, neither sensation nor intellect seems to be at work. Already Aristotle posited a kind of intermediary psychological faculty, the *phantasia*—often translated 'imagination', though its functions are wider than that would suggest. A further significant development came with ancient medical texts, which argued for locating such functions as memory and imagination in specific parts of the brain. This link to a physical organ, and the fact that imagination, memory, and certain lower kinds of thought have to do with particulars rather than universals, suggests associating these cognitive abilities more with sensation than with intellection. That step was taken in dramatic fashion by Avicenna, who devised a scheme of five 'inner senses', all seated in the brain: common sense (for bringing together properties grasped by more than one sense into a single experience), memory, retentive and compositive imagination (which respectively store and manipulate images gleaned from sensation), and estimation (*wahm*). Estimation allows humans, and also non-human animals, to perceive features of our environment that are not graspable by the external senses. Avicenna gave the example of a sheep using its estimative faculty to perceive that a wolf is hostile. This explains why it runs from the wolf, something we could not account for just by invoking its ability to see or hear the wolf. Useful though it is, estimation can also give rise to misconceptions about the world—indeed the Arabic *wahm* can also mean "erroneous impression".

Maimonides. One might be surprised to find these Muslims and Jews claiming that prophecy results from chance suitability in certain people, rather than being a gift sent specifically by God. Yet Maimonides took the naturalist account so seriously that he thought God would have to perform a miracle to *prevent* someone from receiving prophetic insight if that person were apt to receive it. Of course, prophecy remains a sign of divine providence, which ensures that the cosmic order will yield prophets because they are needed by their fellow humans. But this is the same sort of providence manifested by the regularity and good design of the natural world in general: it guarantees that there is prophecy, without determining where and when a particular prophet will arise.

Knowledge by presence

Philosophers too can have powerful imaginations. One example was Suhrawardī, as we can see from his account of a dream vision he enjoyed, in which Aristotle himself appeared and shared some novel insights about knowledge. Before his dream, Suhrawardī was in thrall to the traditional account of knowledge according to which we know things by subsuming them under universals. For instance, knowing that a giraffe is tall means representing it to ourselves as having the feature 'tallness', which can also belong to other things. In the dream, Aristotle chastises Suhrawardī for this naive (and ironically, Aristotelian) epistemological theory. The dream Aristotle seems to have been reading Avicenna, since he gives the counterexample of self-knowledge. When you know yourself, you are not grasping yourself by means of some universally applicable description or property, or through a representation. This is unnecessary, since the self and what it is grasping are one and the same thing.

Perhaps we could admit that self-knowledge is unique in this respect, while insisting that other kinds of knowledge do involve universal representations. But Aristotle is having none of this. He persuades Suhrawardī that our knowledge must be grounded in a direct grasp of particular things. We must know particulars in order to know about universals, not the other way around. We've seen that more Aristotelian philosophers, like al-Fārābī, Avicenna and Averroes, were likewise troubled by the transition from experience of particular things to universal knowledge. Still, they never gave up on the idea that true knowledge must have a universal character. Suhrawardī's dream Aristotle encourages him to abandon this conviction. When we grasp a particular thing, for instance by seeing it, then that particular is 'present' to our soul. Intellection is nothing but the 'presence' of the same thing abstracted from matter.

So it was that Suhrawardī arrived at a new epistemic theory, the doctrine of 'knowledge by presence (*al-'ilm al-ḥudūrī*)'. No longer is self-awareness an anomalous kind of knowing, as it arguably was in Avicenna. If knowledge is the presence of things to the soul, then our access to our own souls through self-awareness is a paradigm case of knowledge. For the soul is above all present to itself. Suhrawardī's view has clear links to Islamic mysticism (see Box 17). If knowledge is the presence of an object to the knower, then the sort of intuitive vision that sufis enjoyed, in which God simply 'revealed' Himself to them, is just another example of knowledge, albeit with a more exalted object. Indeed Suhrawardī made use of sufi imagery to describe what is happening in knowledge by presence, for instance by talking of vision as 'the absence of a veil' between the eye and the thing seen. One of his leading commentators, Quṭb al-Dīn al-Shīrāzī, likewise said that the Illuminationist philosophy as a whole is a matter of 'unveiling (*kashf*)... based on revelation and intuition'.

Suhrawardī also claimed a degree of mystical insight for himself and his philosophy. On this basis, unlike Avicenna and like-minded thinkers, Suhrawardī accepted the existence of Platonic Forms. He pointed to the direct insight of Forms granted to many sages, including of course Plato himself. Notwithstanding these connections to mysticism, Suhrawardī's

Box 17 Rūmī on intellect and soul

One might expect mystically inclined authors to downplay the role of 'intellect' in knowing God, since the term has connotations of discursive, even scientific knowledge. Yet the poems of Rūmī, famous for their description of the mystic's passionate love, also speak of intellectual knowledge. He spoke of participation in a 'universal intellect' that grasps God's reality, and of turning the heart into a perfectly polished mirror that reflects the presence of God. In keeping with this, Rūmī frequently urged his readers to follow 'intellect (*'aql*)' in preference to the 'soul (*nafs*)'. Because the two Arabic words are respectively masculine and feminine in gender, he represented this opposition as a contrast between male and female, for instance by talking of intellect as Adam and soul as Eve. Preferring intellect means restraining the soul and its desires. In the end, we must give up even our conception of ourselves as independently existing, discrete things. For this self-conception 'veils' the true unity of ourselves with God. The sufi 'annihilation (*fanā'*)' of the self thus involves abandoning the values of everyday life, whether this be a matter of physical desire or interpersonal relationships, and focusing our desire on God alone.

theory would in some respects seem more familiar to modern-day epistemologists than the theory of 'the Peripatetics' would. For one thing, most philosophers nowadays assume as a matter of course that we do have knowledge in the strict sense concerning particulars. Suhrawardī's theory of perception also resembles the contemporary epistemological position called 'naive realism'—the view that perceived objects are simply 'given' or 'immediate' to us, without the need for any representation.

Centuries after Suhrawardī, his ideas were taken up by a self-styled heir to his 'Illuminationist' philosophy, Mullā Ṣadrā. Ṣadrā's epistemology draws on his version of the sufis' 'unity of existence', modified through the notion of *tashkīk*: a gradation of intensity within that unity, with each existent constantly changing in its substance as it strives towards the perfect existence that is God. The soul too is subject to this sort of change, and one way that it changes is by knowing things. Ṣadrā agreed with Suhrawardī that knowledge is not a matter of representing external things within the soul after some process of abstraction. Rather, it is for things to be 'present' to the soul. According to Ṣadrā, this means precisely that the soul actually *becomes* the thing it is knowing. The soul does not, of course, thereby become identical with the physical object it is knowing, but it does become identical with the intelligible nature of that object. In this way, Ṣadrā took forward Suhrawardī's insight that grasping the self is a paradigm case of knowledge. In fact, there is no longer any distinction between the two at all. For the soul to know (say) about giraffes is simply for it to know itself, once it has become identical with the intelligible nature of giraffes.

Chapter 6
Ethics and politics

We have now considered how the phenomenon of prophecy was fitted into epistemological theories in the Islamic world. But some prophets do not just know things that the rest of us don't, they also bring a revealed law. This is foundational for both Judaism and Islam, and has posed a further set of questions for philosophers. They sought to reconcile the religious norms laid down in the religious law with the ethical and political norms established by unaided human reason. In articulating those rational norms, thinkers of the Islamic world drew on ideas from the classical tradition. Arabic works on ethics were inspired by two sources in particular: as usual Aristotle, and also Galen, who was himself influenced by Plato and the Stoics. In politics, the most prominent idea to come from the Greeks was Plato's ideal of the philosopher-king. Could such ideas be shown to agree with the teachings of the Qur'ān or the Jewish law? Or did the religious sources effectively render the Hellenic inheritance superfluous?

The state of the soul

Although Aristotle's *Nicomachean Ethics* is the most famous ancient ethical treatise, and was translated into Arabic in the formative period, the early tradition of Hellenizing ethics in the Islamic world was not dominated by Aristotle. A good deal of 'popular' moralistic material came into Arabic from Greek and other languages. This was probably the most widespread sort of secular ethical literature in Arabic (see further Box 18). It included collections of sayings ('wisdom literature') ascribed to famous figures, including ancient philosophers; 'mirrors for princes', like the famous *Kalīla wa-Dimna*, a book of animal-based fables translated from Sanskrit by way of Persian; and books of practical advice, for instance a work on household management by the otherwise obscure Roman-era philosopher Bryson.

Box 18 *Adab* and philosophy

In the formative period, there were highly specialized philosophers like al-Fārābī and the members of the Baghdad school. But philosophical material had a far wider dispersion in upper-class society through the refined activity known collectively as *adab*. Sometimes translated as 'belles-lettres', *adab* showed off an author's linguistic skill, wit, and good taste. Such authors occasionally criticized the *falāsifa* and their beloved Greek sources. In one much-quoted passage, the greatest exponent of *adab*, al-Jāḥiẓ (d. 868–9), expressed his scepticism about the prospects of translating Greek successfully into Arabic. He also mocked al-Kindī in a book of comic anecdotes about misers. Yet al-Jāḥiẓ has aptly been called a 'bibliomaniac', and his wide reading made him familiar with Greek ideas and deeply knowledgeable about early *kalām*. Later *adab* authors, such as al-Tawḥīdī (d. 1023), depict a literary salon culture in which it was the done thing to sprinkle quotations from Greek philosophers into one's dinner conversation. But we should not rule out a more serious engagement with philosophy on the part of these literary stylists. Al-Tawḥīdī was a multi-dimensional figure, a scribe and court intellectual who exchanged views with Miskawayh, wrote an overview of the intellectual sciences, and was attracted to Platonist philosophy and sufism.

As early as al-Kindī, we see how these sub-genres were being received and interwoven. One of his works is a collection of remarks supposedly made by Socrates, who was confused in the Arabic tradition with Diogenes the Cynic (for instance al-Kindī has Socrates living in a wine jar). Another is a work of advice aimed at an aristocratic audience, if not actual royalty, which explains how to avoid becoming sad. Towards this end, al-Kindī invoked philosophical doctrine, advising us not to value physical things, since unlike intelligible objects they are subject to change and destruction. Yet he also quoted from wisdom literature, including a story about Alexander the Great, repeating sayings of Socrates, and elaborating on a classical allegory found in Epictetus, which compares our earthly life to a temporary disembarkation from a ship: like the passengers, we should be ready to leave at a moment's notice.

By concentrating on ways to forestall sadness, al-Kindī implied that the purpose of writing about ethics is to help the reader to attain peace of mind. This had been the goal of many Hellenistic ethicists, too. Routes to *ataraxia* ('freedom from disturbance') ranged from the restrained hedonism of the Epicureans to the belief-free detachment attained by ancient Sceptics. Neither of these two schools was particularly influential in Arabic, however. More decisive was the impact of the Stoic-flavoured Platonism found in the ethical works of Galen. As the leading authority in medicine, his works were voluminously translated into Arabic, and in the bargain two of his writings on ethics passed into the Islamic world. These ethical treatises too offered a sort of medical care—therapy for the soul, rather than the body. It was a commonplace of Hellenistic ethics to compare peace of mind to physical health, and ethical advice to medicine. For instance Epicurus' ethics were distilled into four recommendations called the 'four-part cure (*tetrapharmakos*)'. The titles of two early Arabic ethical works show that this medical analogy was alive and well in the formative period: *Spiritual Medicine* and *Benefits for Bodies and Souls*.

The first is by Abū Bakr al-Rāzī, notorious for his five eternal principles. His *Spiritual Medicine* found much more favour with subsequent readers than that cosmological theory. It was written as a companion piece to an encyclopedic work on (bodily) medicine. It is an entertaining but ethically demanding treatise, which takes as its starting point Plato's distinction between three parts in the soul, which al-Rāzī knew through Galen. The *Spiritual Medicine* exhorts the reader to subdue the lower two souls, the desiring and irascible faculties, to the higher part, which is the rational soul. It is reason that makes us human, and letting oneself be dominated by the lower, body-dependent souls is in effect living as a beast (see further Box 19). A sign of this is the way that animals go after everything they desire as soon as it is

Box 19 Animal welfare

Given that many of these ethical texts encourage us to suppress our lower 'animal' souls, we might expect them to offer little in the way of sympathy towards real animals. And it is true that animals were often ignored in philosophical literature (unlike in the visual arts: see Figure 8). Yet there were exceptions. A belief in God's mercy is a fundamental tenet of Islam, and theologians sometimes extended this to animals. Some Muʿtazilites postulated that animals might receive food in paradise to recompense them for whatever suffering they had to undergo on earth. Several medieval ethicists, meanwhile, argued for benevolence towards animals. One example is Abū Bakr al-Rāzī's *Philosophical Life*, which contains an impassioned criticism of those who overburden pack animals or enjoy hunting, on the basis that we should show mercy to animals as God shows mercy towards us. Al-Rāzī did allow cruelty towards animals in order to save human life, for instance riding a horse to death to escape an enemy, and said that one may kill predatory creatures, since this is a net gain in terms of animal welfare. Another remarkable text for this topic was produced by a group of philosophers writing in

Box 19 Continued

the 10th century, who adopted the name 'Brethren of Purity (*Ikhwān al-Ṣafā'*)'. Their collection of epistles includes a fable which imagines the animal kingdom bringing an official complaint to the king of the *jinn*, protesting at the treatment they receive from humans. The portrayal of animals here is extremely positive: they are 'monotheists' and 'muslims' who pray to God with their calls, and unlike humans they are free from sin. Nonetheless, the trial is eventually decided in favour of the humans, since it is they alone who can include truly pious, saintly figures among their number. For another example we may turn to Ibn Ṭufayl's island story *Ḥayy ibn Yaqẓān*. At one stage in the narrative, the title character decides to participate in God's providential activity by protecting and nurturing not only animals, but also plants. Ḥayy even becomes a fruitarian, restricting his diet to food he can harvest without killing plants. As in al-Rāzī, the attention paid here to animal welfare is not justified with reference to the intrinsic dignity of animals or anything of the sort. Rather, kindness to animals is a way of carrying out God's will.

presented to them, whereas humans have the ability to refrain from this. Often the *Spiritual Medicine* presents such self-control in hedonistic terms, as an Epicurean might have done. Self-control brings more pleasure and less pain in the long run, for instance by preventing discomfort due to overeating.

But unlike the Epicureans, al-Rāzī was no hedonist. He was simply trying to show that even people focused on desire-satisfaction have good reason to subordinate their desires to rational control. Elsewhere, al-Rāzī made it clear that pleasure has no value at all, since it is nothing but the restoration of the body to a healthy state after it has been in a harmful state, as when we drink to restore our balance of moisture. This is a zero-sum game, since the pleasure attendant on the process is always matched by the deficiency or pain being eliminated. On the other hand, enjoying pleasure is not intrinsically evil, either. Pleasures enjoyed in a controlled and thoughtful way were allowed by al-Rāzī, as we can see from another short work called *The Philosophical Life*. Here he defended himself from the accusation that he failed to live up to the standards set by Socrates, who was famous in the Arabic tradition for being an ascetic (in part because of the confusion of Socrates with Diogenes). Al-Rāzī's response was that Socrates was only an ascetic as a young man. Later he outgrew this and adopted a more mature, moderate lifestyle which included such things as wine-drinking and marriage.

Benefits for Bodies and Souls is by a contemporary of al-Rāzī, who was also an associate of al-Kindī: Abū Zayd al-Balkhī (d. 934). As the title indicates it has two main sections, dealing with physical medicine and ethics. Like al-Kindī and al-Rāzī but within an even more explicit 'medical' frame, al-Balkhī treated his subject as a therapeutic one. All three authors gave advice on avoiding sadness; both al-Rāzī and al-Balkhī discussed a range of other psychological 'maladies' such as excessive anger and envy. As al-Balkhī put it, the advice offered for these conditions is intended to 'keep the soul's faculties in a good and balanced condition', much as a doctor would prescribe drugs or a change in diet to preserve or recover the balance of humours in a patient's body. Al-Balkhī's favourite therapeutic technique was the rehearsal of useful thoughts, which should be constantly called to mind to prevent or remove psychological distress. We should for instance remember that physical things are liable to destruction, and so value them less, anticipating their inevitable disappearance. Al-Rāzī's *Spiritual Medicine* applies this same line of thought even to the loss of loved ones.

If such advice seems unhelpful, the problem may be that one cannot simply argue other people, or oneself, out of having desires. On its own, my rational understanding that my loved ones are mortal has no tendency to make me face the prospect of their deaths with equanimity. In the context of the Platonist tripartite soul, the problem here is that the lower souls are not responsive to the sort of considerations that move the rational soul to form its beliefs. Galen already saw this, and observed that we do many things because of the habits we have formed, rather than on the basis of belief. This means the lower soul must be *habituated* into following the lead of reason, like an animal being tamed. That process results in what he calls 'character traits', a term which in its Arabic version (*akhlāq*) became more or less synonymous with the subject matter of 'ethics'.

Here we find agreement between Galen and the other main Hellenic source on ethics, Aristotle. His *Nicomachean Ethics* likewise argues that virtues are formed by habit, which is why moral education needs to happen already at a young age. One author who noticed the harmony between Galen and Aristotle was Miskawayh. His *Refinement of Character Traits* (*Tahdhīb al-akhlāq*) was the most elaborate and influential ethical treatise of the formative period. It makes extensive use of Aristotle, including his account of virtues as 'means between extremes' (for instance courage is the mean between the vices of cowardice and rashness). It also refers explicitly to the ethical works of Galen. This is typical of Miskawayh, who has no hesitation in combining Aristotelian ethics with doctrine with Plato's tripartite soul alongside advice on child-rearing from Bryson. Also typical is the harmony he sees between all these Greek authors and the teachings of Islam. Not only does the *Refinement* occasionally quote the Qur'ān to show its agreement with Miskawayh's ethical teachings. It also gives the religious law (*sharīʿa*) a specific role within that ethical teaching, by making it responsible for the very habituation we have been discussing: the law 'sets the youth on the straight path, habituates them to admirable actions, and prepares their souls to receive wisdom, to seek the virtues, and to reach human happiness'.

This idea was developed within the context of Judaism by Maimonides. Like Miskawayh, Maimonides was heir to both the 'medicalizing' Galenic ethics and Aristotle's theories. He duly presented vices as diseases caused by reason's failure to dominate the lower soul, and saw the virtues as means between extremes. We get from the former to the latter through rigorous habituation, which is precisely what is offered by the religious law. An obvious example might be that following dietary laws teaches Jews to exert control over their desire for food. Maimonides saw a potential problem here, though. If we turn to the Bible, we often find that the patriarchs are depicted as rather ascetic. Abraham, for example, refrained from looking at his wife's body and from collecting spoils that were justly his after military victory. In the Judeo-Christian tradition, such heroic abnegation has often been taken as a sign of piety and virtue. It may not be required, but it is certainly admirable. On Aristotle's reckoning, though, these acts appear vicious, because they fall short of the appropriate mean with respect to the enjoyment of sex and wealth. Maimonides solved the problem by distinguishing between those who are already secure in their virtuous habits, and those who are still working their way towards perfect virtue. The latter group might rightly impose particularly severe constraints on themselves, all the better to condition themselves not to give in to temptation in the future. This is a policy that was often adopted by the patriarchs, on Maimonides' reckoning, and we should not confuse it with perfectly virtuous comportment.

With his extensive reflection on Hellenic ethical theory, Maimonides makes a vivid contrast with earlier Jewish ethical literature, an outstanding example of which is the *Duties of the Heart* by Baḥya ibn Paqūda (d. *c.*1156). This is another book of advice, devoted to the goal of forming intentions that are pleasing to God rather than eliminating imbalances in the soul. Ibn Paqūda claimed to be innovating here. Many previous authors had dealt with *external* actions, including the ritual observances laid down in the Jewish law. He wanted to teach his readers how to cultivate an *inner* motivation of obedience to God. Ibn Paqūda sought to

8. An image from a manuscript of the book of animal fables, *Kalīla wa Dimna*.

shift the focus of Jewish ethics from actions to intentions. A good intention on its own (which might not come to fruition, if it is thwarted by circumstance) has more value than the good action that is intended. Coincidentally, a similar focus on the 'interior' state of the ethical agent was being promoted at about the same time by Latin Christian medieval thinkers like Peter Abelard.

The soul and the state

In the post-formative period, one of the most widely read philosophical works in any discipline was the *Ethics* (again, *Akhlāq*) *for Nāṣir* written by Naṣīr al-Dīn al-Ṭūsī. Despite the title, the book is not only about ethics. Al-Ṭūsī wanted to cover all branches of 'practical philosophy' as recognized by Aristotle. That meant dealing with ethics, but also household management (the original meaning of 'economics', a word that comes from the

Greek for 'household') and political philosophy. Though the work is not without originality, it makes extensive use of existing materials, turning to Miskawayh for ethics, Bryson and Avicenna concerning the household, and al-Fārābī for political philosophy. In this al-Ṭūsī is in line with modern-day historians, who have recognized al-Fārābī as the most interesting political thinker of the formative period.

His *Principles of the Opinions of the Inhabitants of the Virtuous City* discusses God, cosmology and other issues in natural philosophy, and even prophecy, before turning to an account of the best city. The ideal city is contrasted to cities that pursue defective ends, like wealth or pleasure, and its success is achieved through the presence of a philosopher-ruler, who steers the city's inhabitants towards virtue. In yet another example of the widespread 'medicalization' of ethics, al-Fārābī drew an analogy between the ruler's relationship to the inhabitants' souls and a doctor's relationship to his patients' bodies. Much of this sounds familiar from Greek sources, especially Plato's *Republic*. Yet al-Fārābī's political thought was highly original. Among its innovations was the notion that the ideal ruler is also a prophet, able to convey his knowledge in a form made palatable through the use of imaginative symbols. So the rest of the citizens, despite living in a city run according to philosophical principles, do not need to be philosophers themselves. This is, presumably, why the title of al-Fārābī's work ascribes 'opinions' to the inhabitants, as opposed to full-blown knowledge. Applying his universal knowledge to the particular case before him, the ruler can govern the city in light of the needs of its population and local conditions, for instance climate or other geographical factors. He can also respond to new situations with renewed teachings. So long as he lives and is obeyed, the community will enjoy the fruits of his ideal leadership and be led towards virtue.

But what to do when the prophet dies? Unless the community is lucky enough to find another person of similar qualities, they will have to resort to other forms of guidance. A group of people might be found who collectively possess the abilities and characteristics of the perfect ruler. Failing that, the community must fall back on careful exegesis and interpretation of the law brought originally by the prophet. This is the task of jurisprudence (*fiqh*). Without access to the prophet himself, juridical scholars must comb through his teachings and apply them to novel questions or issues. So long as continuity is somehow preserved, the prophet's knowledge is perpetuated as 'religion (*dīn*)'. Religion is analogous to philosophy, just as revelatory discourse is analogous to demonstrative proof. Like philosophy, it has both a practical and a non-practical part, with the adherents of a virtuous religion adopting the right beliefs concerning actions, and true opinions about God and the world.

Al-Fārābī scrupulously avoided explicitly connecting any of this to Islam. For instance we never find him identifying Muḥammad as an example of a prophet-ruler. The account was intended to be general, applicable to *any* virtuous religion. A similar approach was taken by one of the later thinkers most influenced by him, the Andalusian philosopher Ibn Bājja. In his *Regime of the Solitary*, Ibn Bājja again describes an ideal city and contrasts it to defective cities. The title alludes to the plight of right-thinking persons who find themselves in non-virtuous cities. Such people can attain happiness of a sort, but not the full happiness available to those living in perfect cities. Ibn Bājja calls them 'weeds', because they undermine the city in which they live. They have managed to develop correct ideas, either practical or theoretical, and thus represent a challenge to the convictions that hold sway in their vicious societies. In the *Republic*, Plato had Socrates wonder whether the ideal city he was describing could ever exist in practice, and propose that it could occur if by chance a philosophically minded son would be born to a king. The 'weeds' are Ibn Bājja's answer to the same question. (For a less abstract view of dynastic change, see Box 20.)

9. The sacking of Baghdad during the Mongol invasions.

For Ibn Bājja the 'solitary' philosopher is inevitably a kind of dissident, a living rebuke to the corrupt society around him whose very presence will tend to destabilize that society. Like al-Fārābī, he used the analogy of the doctor, but reserved it for the solitary philosopher in the bad city, since in the perfect city no one has a sick soul. Ibn Bājja's fellow Andalusian Ibn Ṭufayl was more pessimistic about the ability of the philosopher to effect political change. At least, this seems to be the message of the final section of his *Ḥayy ibn Yaqẓān*. After having become an accomplished philosopher and even enjoyed mystical union with God, Ḥayy encounters a visitor named Absal. He travels with him to another island, where the local inhabitants are adherents of a religion that sounds very much like Islam. Though Absal is able to recognize Ḥayy's wisdom, the other inhabitants reject him. Ḥayy realizes sorrowfully that the people are not capable of benefiting from his teachings. They must instead cling to the detailed religious injunctions that regulate their lives, lest they fall into vice.

Box 20 Ibn Khaldūn on dynastic rise and fall

The 14th century was a time of great upheaval in the Islamic world. Plague swept through the lands, as did the warlord Tīmūr (often known as Tamerlane), who pushed Mongol hegemony even further than it had reached in the previous century. Meanwhile in the Western Islamic world, or Maghreb, the Almohads had lost Spain to the Christians and various powers jockeyed for control of North Africa. Witness to it all was Ibn Khaldūn, whose enormous historical work *Kitāb al-ʿIbar* (*The Book of Observations*) begins with a book-length introduction (*Muqaddima*). This sets out Ibn Khaldūn's theory of dynastic cycles, a bold attempt to provide a template for explaining historical events inside and outside the Islamic world. According to his theory, civilizations are routinely toppled by tribal groups who draw on the powerful force of *ʿaṣabiyya*, or 'group solidarity'. Typically, the tribal group will be rootless and nomadic, but will settle down in cities and towns once they have deposed a previous regime. The new sedentary life will soften them within a few generations, paving the way for defeat at the hands of a new challenger. The theory fits the history of Muslim Spain very well: the Iberian peninsula had seen a series of conquests launched from North Africa in previous centuries, with power passing from the remnant of the Umayyad caliphate to feudal kings, then to the Almoravids and finally to the Almohads. This is most likely no coincidence, since Ibn Khaldūn hailed from the Maghreb, having been born in Tunisia. But Ibn Khaldūn applied his account to other cases too, not least the extraordinarily rapid conquests of early Islam.

Suhrawardī put his own distinctive spin on the Platonic idea of a philosopher-king, saying that the rightful caliph is someone who has mastered not only the discursive sort of philosophy practised by the 'Peripatetics' but also the intuitive methods used in

Illuminationism. An Iranian thinker of the early Safavid period, al-Nayrīzī, was unimpressed by these remarks. He speculated that Suhrawardī was trying to lay claim to political power for himself. This accusation is not as outlandish as it may seem, for Suhrawardī was put to death on the orders of Saladin because of the influence he exerted on Saladin's teenaged son. On a less *ad hominem* note, al-Nayrīzī pointed out that there has historically been no correlation between philosophical wisdom and political authority.

For al-Nayrīzī and other Safavid-era philosophers, proper authority instead has its source in divine dispensation. The Prophet, and then the imams recognized in shiite Islam, were sent to provide not only revelation but also leadership for the community. It was thus a thwarting of God's plan when the rightful imam ʿAlī was passed over as caliph. This shiite conception of political legitimacy could readily be combined with al-Fārābī's ideas. After all, he too saw a close connection between prophecy and perfect leadership, and acknowledged the possibility of successors who would be able to carry on this aspect of the prophet's role. So when another shiite philosopher, al-Ṭūsī, made use of al-Fārābī in the political section of his *Ethics for Nāṣir*, he could seamlessly weave shiite allusions into this material. (It has been argued that his *Ethics* bears the hallmarks of specifically Ismāʿīlī shiism, which he espoused at this stage of his career.)

In sunni Islam, there has been more room for debate as to whether political power must ideally be allied to religious authority. Many sunni rulers have asserted this sort of double legitimacy. In the 9th century, when the ʿAbbāsid caliphs demanded assent to the Muʿtazilite position on the Qurʾān's createdness, they were also demanding the right to define the boundaries of acceptable doctrine. We can find a parallel in Christian Europe at about the same time, with Charlemagne stepping into theological controversies over the nature of Christ and the worship of images. The rulers of sunni Islam have rarely gone as far as mandating theological positions in this way. In fact the ʿAbbāsid example discouraged later caliphs from doing so, since the inquisition over the Qurʾān's createdness ultimately became politically unsustainable. It has rather been the religious scholars, or *ʿulamāʾ*, whose expertise in the core Islamic texts and the law has made them the usual arbiters of correct doctrine. When al-Ghazālī accused Avicenna of 'apostasy' and said that he would have merited death for holding his philosophical views, he was speaking as a legal scholar.

Still, religious and political legitimacy have often gone hand in hand. The Ottomans, for example, began as religious warriors (*ghāzīs*), and the sultans were always keen to present themselves as defenders of sunni Islam, against both the powers of Christian Europe and the shiite regime of Safavid Iran. That posture gained in credibility when they successfully took Constantinople, and extended their territory to include the religious sites at Mecca. Ottoman sultans also cultivated close ties to the *ʿulamāʾ*, who formed a powerful legal bureaucracy at the heart of Ottoman society. As these scholars came to form a distinct social class, allied to the sultan and passing on lucrative posts through a system that was more nepotistic than meritocratic, they attracted hostile critique. Reform was urged by the populist Kādīzādeli movement, named after its founder Meḥmed Kādīzāde (d. 1635). Philosophers too were alarmed at the corruption of the Ottoman *ʿulamāʾ*, as we can see in the case of Kātib Çelebi. Though he agreed to this extent with the Kādīzādelis, he was concerned not to throw the baby out with the bathwater. The system of religious schools, or *madrasas*, that educated the *ʿulamāʾ* also provided an institutional context for philosophical and scientific knowledge in the Ottoman empire.

A couple of centuries later, though, some rationalist philosophers would be describing the traditional *madrasa* curriculum as backward, and as a hindrance to social progress. Such criticisms were made in both Ottoman and Indian society, as part of a call to arms in the face of colonialism. Some argued that adopting European political and scientific ideas might reverse the loss of territory and sovereignty. In the Ottoman sphere, two waves of reformers urged this policy: the Young Ottomans and then the Young Turks. The Young Ottomans were broadly careful to recognize the value and standing of both the sultan and the *ʿulamāʾ*, but they argued for political reform, for instance by changing from Ottoman absolutism to something more like a European-style constitutional monarchy. The more radical Young Turks, inspired by European thinkers like Durkheim, Büchner, and Comte, were less afraid to step on traditionalist toes. On the scientific and philosophical front, they embraced materialism and positivism; on the political front, they promoted nationalism, paving the way for the secularist project that would ultimately reach its fruition with the new nation of Turkey in the early 20th century.

These developments opened a new front in the struggle to determine the source of political authority in sunni Islam. On the reckoning of the nationalists and other modernizers, legitimate political leadership could be thoroughly secular. This was not presented as an abandonment of the teachings of Islam, of course. To the contrary, modernizers were eager to point to religious texts and aspects of early Islam that could bolster their political views. Thus the Egyptian scholar Muḥammad ʿAbdūh and his teacher Jamāl al-Dīn al-Afghānī cited the traditional practice of *shūrā*, or consultation among the community, as an Islamic analogue to democratic government. Like Averroes, ʿAbdūh was a jurist who emphasized the social importance of religion. But he was dismissive of the traditional *ʿulamāʾ*, whom he saw as trapped in *taqlīd*, the unthinking acceptance of authority. Along with ʿAbdūh's emphasis on individual reflection and political action went a rejection of fatalism, the view that all things are preordained by God. An article in the journal produced by ʿAbdūh along with his teacher al-Afghānī angrily rebutted the European conception of Islam as a fatalist religion. ʿAbdūh worried that fatalism could lead to quietism, since it implies that the current state of political affairs has, along with everything else, been decreed by God. Fatalists are bound to assume that if things are meant to change, then God will ensure that they do: an attitude inimical to the political engagement urged by the modernizers (see also Box 21).

Box 21 The political context of the *kalām* debate over human action

It was nothing new when early 20th century modernizers complained about the political consequences of theological fatalism. Debates over human action and free will had always been politicized. One of the defining features of Muʿtazilism was its stance on the Muslim who commits a grave sin: such a sinner is neither a 'believer' nor a 'hypocrite' but in an 'intermediate position'. This apparently rather obscure teaching was offered as a compromise solution for a highly politicized issue. Some Muslims, notably the Khārijites, believed that those who had sinned through their political actions had effectively exiled themselves from the Muslim community, justifying military action against them. This led to violent schism, which the more tolerant Muʿtazilite formula was designed to avoid. The same goes for the notorious Ashʿarite teaching on human freedom, according to which God 'creates' human actions but the human agent 'acquires' them. The question here was whether God determines all events in the created world or whether humans have some scope for undetermined action. As ʿAbdūh would argue much later, a determinist position could easily be taken to legitimize existing political rule, since that rule has been determined by God. (Already the Umayyad dynasty cultivated an explicit link between their rule and God's decree, or *qaḍāʾ*.) On the other hand, determinism could be taken to undermine personal responsibility: God decides whether each of us will sin, and we cannot change His decision. Wanting to steer well clear of this consequence, the Muʿtazilites insisted that it would be

Box 21 Continued

unjust for God to punish sinners if they were unfree. But this assumes that we humans are in a position to say what God can do within the bounds of justice. That seemed presumptuous to the Ashʿarites, who believed that God's choices define what is just, rather than adhering to some external standard of right and wrong. Instead, they suggested a compromise of their own: humans are not in a position to 'create' their actions or anything else, but they still retain responsibility for what they do through their 'acquisition (*kasb*)' of the actions God assigns to them.

At about the same time, similar views were being put forward by Muslim rationalists in India. Indian thinkers of the late 19th and early 20th centuries, like Sayyid Aḥmad Khān and Muḥammad Iqbāl, agreed with contemporary Ottoman modernizers that the Islamic world should not just welcome European science, but claim priority of discovery. Iqbāl argued that the medieval optical theorist Ibn al-Haytham (d. 1039) should take credit for pioneering experimental method, and that Miskawayh had anticipated Darwinian evolutionary theory. (Similarly, ʿAbdūh believed he could find evolution adumbrated in the Qurʾān.) More generally, Iqbāl saw Islam as a distinctively empirical religion. He referred to the Qurʾān's repeated calls to observe nature and see it as the proof of God's might and wisdom—texts cited centuries earlier in Averroes' *Decisive Treatise* to prove the harmony of Islam and Aristotelian philosophy. Iqbāl was here influenced by the ideas of the German philosopher Friedrich Nietzsche, whom he had studied in Europe. Iqbāl followed Nietzsche's idea that one should value this world rather than despising it, and agreed with him that world-denying tendencies were rife in Judeo-Christianity. Islam is different, though. It 'says "yes" to the world' and with its 'reverence for the actual' has encouraged Muslims to become 'the founders of modern science'.

Nor did Iqbāl see any conflict between science and mysticism. Arguing against another Western thinker, William James, Iqbāl rejected the idea that mystical consciousness is wholly different in kind from empirical knowledge. The mystic simply grasps all at once what the scientist is grasping one part at a time. This commitment to the ultimate unity of knowledge is something Iqbāl shared with the earlier Indian sufi thinker Shāh Walī Allāh. But Iqbāl's Nietzschean distaste for world-denying philosophies meant dismissing the practice of ascetic withdrawal from the world as 'false sufism'. Islam rather calls us to engage with the world, through both empirical science and political action. For Iqbāl the political ideals of Islam (which he equated with *tawḥīd*: 'oneness' or 'monotheism') are equality, solidarity, and freedom. Such ideals would be realized not by separating religion from politics, but by bringing all Muslims into a unified global community, crossing all boundaries of ethnicity and nation. Iqbāl was therefore critical of the sort of nationalist project urged by the Young Turks and by some of his contemporaries in India.

One political issue that increasingly came to the fore at this time was the rights of women. The reforms unleashed in the 19th-century Ottoman empire opened up new opportunities for women, including the chance to publish in journals and magazines. This is not to say that Muslim women had previously been entirely excluded from intellectual activities. Religious learning had often been passed from one generation to the next by women scholars, who played a major role in the transmission of the *ḥadīth* (reports about the Prophet). This began already with the Prophet's favourite wife, 'Ā'isha, one of the most prolific original witnesses of *ḥadīth*. Other women followed her example, observing the mandate that women should emulate the Prophet's wives. In sufism, too, women played a significant role. Indeed one of the earliest significant mystics was female: Rābiʿa, who pioneered the idea that the sufi's relationship to God is one of love and erotic longing, a central theme in the poetry of Rūmī.

More recently, the position of women in Islam has been interrogated by thinkers like the sociologist and feminist Fatema Mernissi. She has done empirical research, with extensive interviews of women in Morocco, and also built a case for gender equality by returning to the core texts of Islam. In her work *Beyond the Veil*, first published in 1973, she argued that Islamic society has long been gripped by a fear of women's power over men. Such practices as polygamy, veiling, and the repudiation of wives are a collective 'strategy for containing [women's] power'. Mernissi contrasted this to the way that women have been seen as passive and weak in the European tradition, not least by Sigmund Freud (in making this point, she compared the Freudian understanding of women to remarks by al-Ghazālī). On Mernissi's reading the traditional treatment of women represents a distortion of the original teaching of Islam. Using the techniques of *ḥadīth* scholarship, she argued that certain Prophetic reports used to justify this treatment (for instance 'those who entrust their affairs to a woman will never know prosperity') are unsound. They have been treated as trustworthy only because the misogynistic leanings of influential Muslim men led them to suppress the egalitarian aspects of the Islamic revelation.

Mernissi and other liberal Muslim thinkers have frequently presented their reformist agenda as a return to the original teachings of Islam. Another example is Sayyid Aḥmad Khān's assessment of polygamy. Admittedly, Islam does allow a man to marry as many as four wives. Yet it also requires that the wives be treated with total equality. Khān argued that, since this is in practice impossible, polygamy is effectively prohibited in Islam after all. Ironically, a similar strategy of returning to the origins of Islam has also been adopted by far more socially conservative Muslims. For them a major inspiration has been Ibn Taymiyya, whose 'salafist' approach to jurisprudence took its name from the *salaf*, or first generations of Muslims. It would seem that for some centuries, Ibn Taymiyya's influence was rather limited, but more recently he has probably played a more prominent role in political discourse in the Islamic world than any of the other historical figures discussed in this book.

Yet quite a few figures from previous centuries have continued to live on in contemporary political and philosophical discussion. Mullā Ṣadrā's philosophy has had a particularly vibrant legacy in Iran. He influenced no less a political actor than the Ayatollah Khomeini, spiritual leader of the Iranian revolution, though the relationship between this revolution and the Ṣadrean philosophy of a 20th-century Iranian thinker like Ṭabāṭabāʾī is a matter of dispute. Even relatively minor figures have had a surprisingly powerful presence in recent intellectual developments. An example would be Miskawayh. We saw just now that Iqbāl gave him credit for advancing a precursor of the theory of evolution; his work was also taught at al-Azhar University in Cairo by ʿAbdūh; and he has been a source of inspiration for the Algerian thinker Mohammed Arkoun (d. 2010).

All of this is another reason to abandon the usual understanding of philosophy in the Islamic world as a branch of medieval philosophy. Certainly there were fascinating Muslim thinkers—and fascinating Christian and Jewish thinkers living among Muslims—in the medieval period. But the story of philosophy's development in the lands of Islam after medieval times is one of continuity, not rupture or oblivion. 'Medieval' thinkers have never stopped being relevant, even if only indirectly, thanks to many generations of epitomizers, commentators, super-commentators, and critics. For all the innovation, all the pointed critique of predecessors, philosophy in the Islamic world has always remembered its own history.

Philosophy in the Islamic World: timeline

All dates AD. Dates in the Muslim calendar are approximately the dates given here, minus 622—adjustment is needed, since the Muslim calendar year is a slightly different length. For historical events, use has been made of G. Endress, *Der Islam in Daten* (Munich: 2006).

Historical events	*Dates of thinkers (death dates, unless otherwise specified)*
622 Emigration of Muslims to Medina, which marks start of Islamic calendar	
632 Death of the Prophet Muḥammad	
636 Muslim army defeats Byzantines at the Battle of Yarmūk	
661 Murder of ʿAlī, cousin and son-in-law of the Prophet, seen as rightful leader by shiite Muslims	
661 Beginning of Umayyad caliphate	
749 Beginning of ʿAbbāsid caliphate	748 Wāṣil ibn ʿAṭāʾ
754–775 Caliphate of al-Manṣūr	
786–809 Caliphate of Hārūn al-Rashīd	
813–833 Caliphate of al-Maʾmūn	
836 Caliph al-Muʿtaṣim relocates capital from Baghdad to Samarra	

855 Death of Aḥmad ibn Ḥanbal	849 Abū-l Hudhayl
	after 870 al-Kindī
	873 Ḥunayn ibn Isḥāq
900 Sāmānid takeover of Khurāsān	*c.*907 Isaac Israeli
	922 al-Ḥallāj
929 ʿAbd al-Raḥmān III declared caliph in Islamic Spain	925 Abū Bakr al-Rāzī
	935/6 al-Ashʿarī
	940 Abū Bishr Mattā
945 Būyids take power in Iraq	942 Saadia Gaon
	950/1 al-Fārābī
973 Establishment of Cairo as capital of the Fāṭimids	
998–1030 Incursion of Maḥmūd of Ghazna into northwest India; al-Bīrūnī writes about Indian culture	1030 Miskawayh
1031 Last Umayyad caliph in Spain followed by political fragmentation	1037 Avicenna
	1039 Ibn al-Haytham
1055 Seljuqs take power in Baghdad	1057/8 Ibn Gabirol
	1063 Ibn Ḥazm
1076 End of Fāṭimid dynasty in Egypt	
1090 Beginning of Almoravid rule in Spain	
1099 The First Crusade culminates in a massacre at Jerusalem	1111 al-Ghazālī
1118 Disintegration of Seljuk state	1139 Ibn Bājja
1147 Defeat of Almoravids by Almohads	*c.*1156 Baḥya ibn Paqūda
1148 Second Crusade ends in failure	1160's Abū l-Barakāt al-Baghdādī
1171 Saladin founds the Ayyubid sultanate	1167 Abraham ibn Ezra

	1180 Abraham ibn Daud
1187 Saladin smashes crusader army at the Battle of Ḥaṭṭīn	1185 Ibn Ṭufayl
1193 Death of Saladin	1191 Suhrawardī
	1198 Averroes
	1204 Maimonides
1220 Mongols attack Khurāsān	1210 Fakhr al-Dīn al-Rāzī
1227 Death of Genghis Khan	
1242 Mongols attack Anatolia	1240 Ibn ʿArabī
1258 Mongols take Baghdad under leadership of Hülegü	1273 Rūmī
	1274 al-Qūnawī and Naṣīr al-Dīn al-Ṭūsī
1265–1271 Mamluks dislodge Crusaders from Palestine and Syria	1276 Najm al-Dīn al-Kātibī
	1284 Ibn Kammūna
1303 Mamluks end Mongol advance in Syria	1311 Quṭb al-Dīn al-Shīrāzī
1326 Death of Osman, founder of Ottoman dynasty	1328 Ibn Taymiyya
	1344 Gersonides
1351–1414 Tughluq dynasty in Delhi	1355 al-Ījī
1389 Ottomans victorious at Battle of Kosovo	1390 al-Taftazānī
1398 Tīmūr's Mongols invade northern India	
1402 Tīmūr defeats Ottomans at Ankara	
1405 Death of Tīmūr	1406 Ibn Khaldūn
	1411/11 Ḥasdai Crescas
1425 Building of observatory at Samarqand	
1453 Constantinople falls to Ottomans	1474 ʿAlāʾ al-Dīn al-Qūshjī

	1488 Khojazāda
1492 Muslims and Jews expelled from Spain	1498 Ṣadr al-Dīn al-Dashtakī
	1501 Jalāl al-Dīn al-Dawānī
1501–1524 Savafids established in Azerbaijan and Iran	1508 Isaac Abravanel
1517 Ottomans defeat Mamluks in Egypt	
1529 First siege of Vienna by Ottomans	
1524–1576 Reign of Tahmāsp in Iran	1541 Ghiyāth al-Dīn al-Dashtakī
1565 Uniting of Muslim states in Dekkan	
1566 Death of Suleyman the Magnificent	
1588–1629 Expansion of Safavids under Shāh ʿAbbās	1631 Mīr Dāmād
1635 Death of Meḥmed Kādīzāde, leader of a popular religious movement in the Ottoman empire	1640 Mullā Ṣadrā
	1652 Maḥmūd Jawnpūrī
	1657 Kātib Çelebi
1683 Second siege of Vienna	1659 Dārā Shikūh
1707 Death of Mughal emperor Aurangzīb	
1722 End of effective Safavid rule	1731 ʿAbd al-Ghanī al-Nābulusī
	1762 Shāh Walī Allāh
1738 Invasion of India by Nādir Shāh	1748 Niẓām al-Dīn Sihālavī
1757 British take control of Calcutta	
1798–1801 Napoleon invades Egypt	
1804–1813 Russian-Iranian war	
1805–1848 Muḥammad ʿAlī reigns in Egypt	

1858 End of Mughal dynasty	1861 Faḍl al-Ḥaqq al-Khayrabādī
1865 Founding of the Young Turks	
1876 Written constitution as climax of *tanzimat* reforms	1878 Sabzawārī
1882 British invade Egypt	1905 Muḥammad ʿAbdūh
1898 Death of Sayyid Aḥmad Khān, modernist founder of Aligarh University	
1915 Armenian genocide in Turkey	
1916 Sykes-Picot Agreement formalizes post-Ottoman arrangements	
1923 Founding of Turkish Republic	
1925 End of Qajar rule in India	1924 Ziya Gökalp
	1932 Abdullah Cevdet
1938 Death of Mustafa Kemal (Atatürk)	1938 Muḥammad Iqbāl
1952 Egyptian revolution	born 1940 Fatema Mernissi
1979 Iranian revolution	1981 Ṭabāṭabāʾī

Further reading

The suggested readings for individual chapters consist of a small number of suggested primary sources in translation. Each suggested text is followed by one or two items of relevant secondary literature, marked with bullet points.

General works: primary sources in translation

M. A. Khalidi (ed.), *Medieval Islamic Philosophical Writings* (Cambridge: 2005).

C. Manekin (ed.), *Medieval Jewish Philosophical Writings* (Cambridge: 2007).

J. McGinnis and D. C. Reisman (ed. and trans.), *Classical Arabic Philosophy: An Anthology of Sources* (Indianapolis: 2007).

J. Renard (ed.), *Islamic Theological Themes: A Primary Source Reader* (Oakland: 2014).

General works: secondary sources

P. Adamson, *A History of Philosophy without any Gaps: Philosophy in the Islamic World* (Oxford: forthcoming).

P. Adamson and R. C. Taylor (eds), *The Cambridge Companion to Arabic Philosophy* (Cambridge: 2005).

H. Daiber, *Bibliography of Islamic Philosophy*, 2 vols (Leiden: 1999; supplement 2007).

D. H. Frank and O. Leaman (eds), *History of Jewish Philosophy* (London: 1997).

D. H. Frank and O. Leaman (eds), *The Cambridge Companion to Medieval Jewish Philosophy* (Cambridge: 2003).

S. H. Nasr and O. Leaman (eds), *History of Islamic Philosophy*, 2 vols (London: 1996).

U. Rudolph (ed.) *Grundriss der Geschichte der Philosophie. Philosophie in der islamischen Welt, Bd.1: 8.-10. Jahrhundert* (Basel: 2012).

T. Winter, *The Cambridge Companion to Classical Islamic Theology* (Cambridge: 2008).

Chapter 2: Reason and revelation

Suggested text: Renard, *Islamic Theological Themes* [see above], 135–214.

- P. Adamson, 'Arabic Philosophy and Theology Before Avicenna', in J. Marenbon (ed.), *The Oxford Handbook of Medieval Philosophy* (Oxford: 2012), 58–82.
- R. M. Frank, *Early Islamic Theology: The Muʿtazilites and al-Ashʿarī* (Aldershot: 2007).

Suggested text: Averroes, *Decisive Treatise*, in McGinnis and Reisman, *Classical Arabic Philosophy* [see above], 309–30.

- R. C. Taylor, 'Truth Does Not Contradict Truth: Averroes and the Unity of Truth', *Topoi* 19 (2000), 3–16.

Suggested text: Ibn al-ʿArabī, *The Ringstones of Wisdom*, trans. C. K. Dagli (Chicago: 2004).

- W. C. Chittick, *The Sufi Path of Knowledge: Ibn al-ʿArabī's Metaphysics of Imagination* (Albany: 1989).

Suggested text: W. Hallaq (trans.), *Ibn Taymiyya Against the Greek Logicians* (Oxford: 1993).

- A. von Kügelgen, 'The Poison of Philosophy: Ibn Taymiyya's Struggle for and Against Reason', in B. Krawietz and G. Tamer (eds), *Islamic Theology, Philosophy and Law: Debating Ibn Taymiyya and Ibn Qayyim al-Jawziyya* (Berlin: 2013), 253–328.

Chapter 3: God and being

Suggested text: al-Kindī's *On First Philosophy*, in P. Adamson and P. E. Pormann (trans.), *The Philosophical Works of al-Kindī* (Karachi: 2012).

- P. Adamson, *al-Kindī* (New York: 2007).

Suggested text: 'Avicenna on God as the Necessary Existent', in McGinnis and Reisman, *Classical Arabic Philosophy* [see above], 211–19.

- P. Adamson, 'From the Necessary Existent to God', in P. Adamson (ed.), *Interpreting Avicenna* (Cambridge: 2013).
- J. McGinnis, *Avicenna* (New York: 2010).

Suggested text: Mullā Ṣadrā's *The Wisdom of the Throne*, trans. J. W. Morris (Princeton: 1981).

- I. Kalin, *Knowledge in Later Islamic Philosophy: Mullā Ṣadrā on Existence, Intellect and Intuition* (New York: 2010).
- F. Rahman, *The Philosophy of Mullā Ṣadrā* (Albany: 1975).
- S. Rizvi, *Mullā Ṣadra and Metaphysics: Modulation of Being* (London: 2009).

Chapter 4: Eternity

Suggested text: al-Ghazālī's *Incoherence of the Philosophers*, trans. M. E. Marmura (Provo: 1997).

- F. Griffel, *Al-Ghazālī's Philosophical Theology* (New York: 2009).
- T. Kukkonen, 'Possible Worlds in the *Tahāfut al-Falāsifa*: al-Ghazālī on Creation and Contingency', *Journal of the History of Philosophy* 38 (2000), 479–502.

Suggested text: Maimonides, *Guide for the Perplexed*, trans. S. Pines (Chicago: 1963).

- K. Seeskin, *Maimonides on the Origin of the World* (Cambridge: 2005).

Chapter 5: Knowledge

Suggested text: al-Fārābī, *Letter on the Intellect*, in McGinnis and Reisman, *Classical Arabic Philosophy* [see above], 68–78.

- D. L. Black, 'Knowledge *('ilm)* and Certitude *(yaqīn)* in al-Fārābī's Epistemology', *Arabic Sciences and Philosophy* 16 (2006), 11–46.

Suggested text: 'Avicenna's flying man argument', in McGinnis and Reisman, *Classical Arabic Philosophy* [see above], 175–9.

- M. E. Marmura, 'Avicenna's "Flying Man" in Context', *Monist* 69 (1986), 383–95.

Suggested text: Suhrawardī on knowledge by presence, in J. Walbridge and H. Ziai (ed. and trans.), *Suhrawardī: The Philosophy of Illumination* (Provo: 1999), 76–83; 104–6.

- H. Eichner, '"Knowledge by Presence", Apperception in the Mind–Body Relationship', in P. Adamson (ed.), *The Age of Averroes* (London: 2011), 117–40.
- J. Kaukua, *Self-Awareness in Islamic Philosophy: Avicenna and Beyond* (Cambridge: 2015).

Chapter 6: Ethics and politics

Suggested text: al-Rāzī, *The Philosopher's Way of Life*, in McGinnis and Reisman, *Classical Arabic Philosophy* [see above], 36–44.

- T.-A. Druart, 'Al-Rāzī's Conception of the Soul: Psychological Background to his Ethics', *Medieval Philosophy and Theology* 5 (1996), 245–63.

Suggested text: al-Fārābī, *Book of Religion*, C. E. Butterworth (trans.), *Alfarabi: The Political Writings* (Ithaca: 2001), 93–113.

- T.-A. Druart (1996), 'Al-Fārābī, Ethics and First Intelligibles', *Documenti e studi sulla tradizione filosofica medievale* 7 (1996), 403–23.

Suggested text: al-Ṭūsī, *Ethics for al-Nāṣir*, in G. M. Wickens (trans.), *The Nasirean Ethics* (London: 1964).

- W. Madelung, 'Naṣīr al-Dīn Ṭūsī's Ethics Between Philosophy, Shiʿism, and Sufism', in R. G. Hovannisian (ed.) *Ethics in Islam* (Malibu: 1985), 85–101.

Suggested text: M. Iqbāl, *The Reconstruction of Religious Thought in Islam* (London: 1934).

- I. S. Sevea, *The Political Philosophy of Muhammad Iqbal* (Cambridge: 2012).

Index

A

B

C

D

E

F

G

M

N

O

P

Q

ANCIENT EGYPT

A Very Short Introduction

Ian Shaw

The ancient Egyptians are an enduring source of fascination – mummies and pyramids, curses and rituals have captured the imagination of generations. We all have a mental picture of ancient Egypt, but is it the right one? How much do we really know about this great civilization?

In this absorbing introduction, Ian Shaw describes how our current ideas about Egypt are based not only on the thrilling discoveries made by early Egyptologists but also on fascinating new kinds of evidence produced by modern scientific and linguistic analyses. He also explores the changing influences on our responses to these finds, through such media as literature, cinema and contemporary art. Each chapter deals with a different aspect of ancient Egypt, from despotic pharaohs to dismembered bodies, and from hieroglyphs to animal-headed gods.

BIBLICAL ARCHAEOLOGY

A Very Short Introduction

Eric H. Cline

Archaeologist Eric H. Cline here offers a complete overview of this exciting field. He discusses the early pioneers, the origins of biblical archaeology as a discipline, and the major controversies that first prompted explorers to go in search of sites that would "prove" the Bible. He then surveys some of the most well-known modern archaeologists, the sites that are essential sources of knowledge for biblical archaeology, and some of the most important discoveries that have been made in the last half century, including the Dead Sea Scrolls and the Tel Dan Stele.

www.oup.com/vsi

Classical Mythology

A Very Short Introduction

Helen Morales

From Zeus and Europa, to Diana, Pan, and Prometheus, the myths of ancient Greece and Rome seem to exert a timeless power over us. But what do those myths represent, and why are they so enduringly fascinating? This imaginative and stimulating *Very Short Introduction* is a wide-ranging account, examining how classical myths are used and understood in both high art and popular culture, taking the reader from the temples of Crete to skyscrapers in New York, and finding classical myths in a variety of unexpected places: from Arabic poetry and Hollywood films, to psychoanalysis, the bible, and New Age spiritualism.

www.oup.com/vsi

FREE SPEECH

A Very Short Introduction

Nigel Warburton

'I disapprove of what you say, but I will defend to the death your right to say it' This slogan, attributed to Voltaire, is frequently quoted by defenders of free speech. Yet it is rare to find anyone prepared to defend all expression in every circumstance, especially if the views expressed incite violence. So where do the limits lie? What is the real value of free speech? Here, Nigel Warburton offers a concise guide to important questions facing modern society about the value and limits of free speech: Where should a civilized society draw the line? Should we be free to offend other people's religion? Are there good grounds for censoring pornography? Has the Internet changed everything? This Very Short Introduction is a thought-provoking, accessible, and up-to-date examination of the liberal assumption that free speech is worth preserving at any cost.

> 'The genius of Nigel Warburton's *Free Speech* lies not only in its extraordinary clarity and incisiveness. Just as important is the way Warburton addresses freedom of speech - and attempts to stifle it - as an issue for the 21st century. More than ever, we need this book.'
>
> **Denis Dutton, University of Canterbury, New Zealand**

www.oup.com/vsi